BLOW BY BLOW

BLOW BY BLOW

A Collection of Steve Blow's

Award-Winning Columns

From The Dallas Morning News

Dallas
Three Forks Press

Three Forks Press
P.O. Box 823461
Dallas, Texas 75382

ISBN 0-9637629-8-2
Library of Congress Card Number: 00-109973

Printed in the United States of America

Contents

On the Soapbox, 69-91

Adventures Fast and Slow, 93-115

TV Preachers, 'Babatists' & Other Fellow Sinners, 117-137

People Stories, 139-157

Family Matters, 159-179

Foreword

I THINK I was upside down in the cockpit of a U.S. Navy F-18 fighter jet, flying with the famed Blue Angels aerobatic team, when the feeling hit me the strongest: "I love my job! I *love* my job!"

It's a realization that comes to me often, sometimes in little ripples of contentment, sometimes in big booming gusts. The ripples usually come in the middle of an interview with some charming old-timer, when I feel so privileged to have a job that lets me just sit and visit. The gusts usually come when my job is allowing me to fulfill some boyhood fantasy, like actually taking the control stick of that fighter jet to fly some loops and rolls.

Oh, there are times when it feels like a job, too—when I have inadvertently offended someone, when it's 20 minutes till deadline and the words just won't come. But most of the time I can't believe my good fortune to have stumbled into this wonderful job. And I can't believe that almost 12 years have passed since I began it. What is represented here is a smattering of columns from the first 10 of those years—about 100 of almost 1,500 columns written during that time.

Weeding out most of those columns was easy. It's amazing how short the shelf life of a column is. I looked back and found myself waxing strongly about some news events that I now barely remember. It was a good reminder not to take today's little controversies too seriously. These, too, will be mostly forgotten in 10 years.

But once the moldy columns had been tossed out, the process got real hard. It's not that the columns are precious to me, but that the people in them are. I feel a real attachment to almost everyone I've written about (with the possible exception of some of those found in the "Rounders and Rascals" chapter). Choosing to leave a column out felt like an act of betrayal. If I did this selection process all over again, I'd probably come up with a whole different mix of columns.

So forgive me if one of your favorites isn't here. I'm always so honored when someone remembers a column I wrote years ago. Or remembers one from yesterday, for that matter. And forgive me if some of these columns don't connect with you. I picked a few for purely sentimental reasons. Mostly, I'm just tickled that anyone wants to read any of these again.

If you want to know the truth, I still can't believe I'm a columnist for *The Dallas Morning News*. "Columnist" is one of those lofty words that belongs only to folks of such talent and stature as the late Paul Crume, who wrote the front-page "Big D" column in *The Dallas Morning News* for many years.

I had no ambition to become a columnist. I was happy as a reporter. But I owe a lot to an editor, Bob Mong, for suggesting that I try my hand at column writing—and for helping me see that a columnist can still be a reporter at heart. The columnist doesn't have to be the star of the show, Bob explained. The columnist's subjects should be. And so I still see myself primarily as a reporter, one simply privileged to write in the more relaxed and casual style of columns.

I have mentioned Bob Mong, so let me start my thank-yous with him. I wouldn't be doing this job without his gentle nudge, and I haven't told him often enough how appreciative I am. Of course, he's now president and general manager of the newspaper, so I guess he's done OK without my show of gratitude. I also say thanks to all the good editors I have had down through the years, but especially to Steve Harris, who has been my editor the longest. He's the best kind of editor—a friend. His editing touch is light but unerring, and I thank him for saving me from myself on several occasions.

I'm feeling especially grateful these days to the college teachers who gave me such a good start in this business. First on the list is Dr. Blanche Prejean, the taskmaster teacher at Tyler Junior College, where I first wandered into a journalism course. She wouldn't tolerate a newspaper lead in passive voice, and I'm a better man for it. At the University of North Texas, Keith Shelton and Roy Moses befriended me and guided me. And department chairman C.E. Shuford scared and inspired me. I thank every teacher who ever put up with me.

Colleagues have also been valuable teachers. Fellow *Morning News* columnist Larry Powell led me around on my very first day as a professional journalist. That was at the late, great *Fort Worth Press*. Scott Parks and I have been cussing and discussing journalism since our days together at North Texas. We continue the discussion today at *The News*. Dave Tarrant is another colleague who knows about good writing and good friendship. And thanks go to my friend Peter Applebome, now of *The New York Times*, who helped broaden my horizons and gave me a journalistic standard to shoot for.

Finally, and mostly, I thank my family. You will see a lot of them in these pages, so I won't belabor the subject here. But I was lucky enough to grow up with a mother who loved words and beauty, a father who modeled kindness and integrity and a big extended family of grandparents, aunts and uncles and cousins who loved learning and lively discussion. Uncle Jan Kent was an especially good influence in that regard, and I'll always be grateful. He helped instill a vital journalist's trait—curiosity. And infinite thanks, of course, to my wonderful, patient, good-humored wife, Lori, and to my children, Allison and Corey. They're better than I deserve.

Steve Blow
October, 2000

BLOW BY BLOW

Bigger 'n Dallas

IN MY VERY first column, the first one you will find here, I confessed my inferiority complex about Dallas. My first relationship with the city was as an awe-struck visitor. And I still feel like a perpetual visitor to the place—the yokel just in from East Texas.

But maybe that's a good perspective for a columnist to keep, always observing with just a touch of the newcomer's amazement. What a treat it has been to explore the city, past and present. Here you will find a mixture of columns from all sorts of corners of the city.

In one of these columns I confessed that I like Dallas more than love it. And I braced for a real backlash. But it never came. Hardly a word. More just a yawn and a "Me, too." That still troubles me. Surely there's more to Dallas than a good place to make money.

I'm still hoping for that ineffable something that pulls us all together as a city, as a place to love.

Fascination of the City
Still 'Bigger 'n Dallas'

FIRST COLUMNS are like first kisses—inevitably self-conscious, awkward and useless indicators of things to come. This is a first column.

Beginning today and on ensuing Mondays, Wednesdays and Fridays, I'll be on your doorstep. OK, on most mornings, you'll probably find me lying in your shrubs. Or you might look out in the gutter.

We will meet here in this corner of the newspaper. I'll have this silly smile frozen on my face. You will have those little black smudges of ink on your fingertips. It'll be great.

Just so that we know a little of what to expect, let's use this first column to introduce ourselves. I've lived in the Dallas area off and on for more than 15 years. Even so, I still feel like a visitor much of the time. I'm not sure why.

Maybe it goes back to childhood. My earliest relationship with Dallas was that of periodic awe-struck visitor.

I grew up 100 miles to the east in Tyler. Dallas was our Big Apple. Think of that! Maybe a crab apple by comparison, but we can't all grow up in New Jersey.

I come from a part of the world in which people actually said bigger 'n Dallas" to mean anything stupendous. Sample conversation: "What did the Grand Canyon look like?" "It's a hole bigger 'n Dallas."

In my youth, the family would load up into the station wagon and head for Dallas to partake of its culture and sophistication. You know—Six Flags, the State Fair, the Ice Capades.

Occasionally we would stop to gawk at the splendor of NorthPark. And we went to the Cotton Bowl a few times when Dad got free tickets at work. All I remember from those games is that Jerry Levias and James Street were good and Notre Dame had nice helmets.

Once we really busted the family budget and came to Dallas to see The Sound of Music, followed by dinner atop the Southland Life Building at the elegant, oh-so-exotic Ports O'Call. It was the first time I encountered finger bowls, which seemed to fly in the face of everything I'd learned about good table manners in East Texas.

What do I remember most about Dallas culture? A nearly naked woman on a billboard. The sign stood for years along R.L. Thornton Freeway out on the eastern edge of town, where a callow youth arriving from East Texas couldn't miss it. The billboard advertised the strip tease artistry of the Tamlo Lounge.

The big, buxom stripper on that billboard stood for me like Dallas' own Statue of Liberty, welcoming me and my yearnings to town.

I never laid eyes on the actual Tamlo Lounge, but in my imagination it defined Dallas and the wild adventure of big-city life. Little did I know.

(I have just looked in the phone book to see if the Tamlo Lounge still exists. It doesn't. But there is a listing for "Tamlo Data Systems." Now that's the wild and wicked Dallas I have come to know.)

Now that I'm older and wiser, I know that there are those who say Big D stands for Dull. Or Data Systems. OK, so maybe insurance and integrated circuits are our glamour industries. And maybe we've got more than our share of the uptight and buttoned-down.

But the city has its charms. I once did a story looking at how Dallas is depicted in the foreign press. My favorite assessment was from a Mexico City magazine: "If New York is the city that never sleeps, Dallas is the city that never fails to give good bank service."

Oh yeah, sing it: I want to wake up in a city that never fails to . . . . My kind of town. And now the banks never fail to give good service even while failing.

So we're not New York, New York. Fine by me.

As the eternal visitor to Dallas, I'm still plenty amazed and amused by what goes on here. I hope that perspective is reflected in future columns.

And let's look at it mathematically. If there are 8 million stories in the Naked City, that still means there must be about a million here in the Dressed-for-Success City.

I plan to find them.

I propose to hold a mirror up to our city, and we'll take a look together—at the funny, the serious, the sad and the silly. We'll investigate the nooks and crannies, and maybe the crooks and nannies.

But enough about me. Tell me a little about you.

January 30, 1989

Sixth Floor opens,
and a circle closes

I FELT A circle being closed this week.

Like everyone of sufficient age, I remember too well the starting point of this circle.

We came back from lunch in the school cafeteria to find our sixth-grade teacher, Mrs. Outlaw, crying at her desk.

She offered no explanation except to say that the principal would be in the classroom shortly to make an announcement.

After whispered consultations between desks, our only guess was that Mrs. Outlaw had been fired.

Soon, Mr. McMillan came into the classroom, looking even more stern than usual.

"President Kennedy was killed in Dallas today," he said.

We were dismissed early from school. I remember standing at our back fence later that afternoon, talking to the kid who lived behind us.

"Did you hear the good news?" he asked with glee.

I have thought of that question often over the years. For a long time I assumed he had heard his parents say it, which was painful to believe. Now I think he simply made the childish leap of logic that if his parents had criticized Kennedy's politics then his death would be a good thing.

Either way, that question was my first inkling that there could be anything other than pure, sweet grief over the tragedy.

It would be years later before I understood the shame and humiliation that Dallas residents felt along with their grief.

I don't think I fully understood until I was grown and a friend from New York told me about his memories of that Friday afternoon. He was in junior high school on Long Island. "We spent the rest of that day having a class discussion about what kind of people must live in Texas, about what kind of people would kill the president."

Of course Dallas didn't kill the president. A sad, angry, alienated young man named Lee Oswald did that.

We hadn't seen many of his type in 1963. We've seen too many since.

But like the flash of an unexpected photograph, the assassination caught Dallas in some highly unflattering poses. Smug, self-righteous, intolerant. We were embarrassed, and rightfully so.

And that's why it was only this week that a fitting historical exhibit on the assassination was opened—more than 25 years after the event.

I never liked the Kennedy Memorial. It's too cold, too forbidding. You come away feeling something of Kennedy's death, but nothing of his life.

It provides no comfort and no context for the tragedy that occurred a few steps away.

It was heartbreaking to see the thousands of people drawn to Dallas each year left standing in the pigeon droppings of Dealey Plaza, staring blankly at the former School Book Depository, reading the small historical marker, trying to make some sense of it all.

A lot of Dallas residents wanted to tear the building down and bury the memories. Fortunately, they did not prevail.

At long last Dallas has found itself able to do the right thing.

On a rainy morning earlier this week, The Sixth Floor, as the exhibit is called, was opened for a media preview. Officials dressed up and made nervous small talk. Construction workers slipped here and there, trying to look inconspicuous as they prepared for Monday's official opening.

I started through the exhibit with notebook in hand and the most professional of intentions. My notebook tells me that the color scheme of the visitors center is a soothing deep green.

But I don't have much more in my notes after that. My tour became a personal experience, not a professional one.

I watched the film clips of Kennedy's speeches, listened to remembrances on the headphones, and saw again the powerful photos from the thousand days of his presidency.

Tears welled in my eyes at several points, and I chewed on the cap of my pen. It's not professional to cry on assignment.

I thought of Mrs. Outlaw and her tears that day in the classroom. I thought of the neighbor kid's foolishness.

And I thought of Dallas' shame and its healing.

I stood at those famous sixth-floor windows, looking out at the rain falling on Elm Street, and I felt a circle close.

February 17, 1989

Bus tour needs
new guide lines

I READ IN the newspaper that Gray Line tours is moving its corporate headquarters from New York to Dallas. That prompted me to wonder what Dallas looks like from a Gray Line bus.

So I forked over $17 one morning last week and took a two-hour Gray Line tour into the Twilight Zone.

Our guide into this new dimension of space and time and Dallas history was "Ronnie." At Dealey Plaza, Ronnie pointed out the route of President Kennedy's motorcade and the sixth-floor window of the former Texas School Book Depository. "However, today we don't actually believe that it was Lee Harvey Oswald in that particular window," he said.

And then Ronnie launched into a long, disjointed discussion of how Oswald couldn't have been in the School Book Depository and Oak Cliff at the same time, how John Connally had court-martialed Oswald a few years before, how Oswald shot at Connally in Dallas shortly before the assassination, how Jack Ruby's cause of death was covered up, and how Lyndon Johnson and J. Edgar Hoover were prime suspects in Kennedy's death.

(For the record, Dallas historian Conover Hunt said, "Oh dear. How do I respond to that? He has obviously mixed up every conceivable detail of the assassination. He did get Oswald's name right.")

At the Dallas County Convention Center, Ronnie directed our attention to the Pioneer Park Cemetery and said, "Three inches under this cemetery, we've got a parking garage. . . . If you park your car here and you get an unwanted guest, you'll know why you got that guest."

(For the record, Convention Center director Jerry Barshop said there is no parking beneath the dead in Dallas.)

At Old City Park, Ronnie discussed the history of shotgun-style houses. "They come from New Orleans. Now when they got to Texas, we called them chicken ranches,' he said. "You know what a chicken ranch is, right?"

A tourist near the front of the bus offered a guess: "A farm with chickens?"

"No, no," Ronnie said, and then someone said a bordello. "Right," Ronnie said. "We've got a famous place down near Austin, Texas. They made a movie about it with Burt Reynolds and Dolly Parton."

(For the record, shotgun houses. . . . Oh, never mind.)

Driving along Central Expressway, Ronnie said, "This was going to be shut down last month, but they didn't do it. They've had a few delays.

"They're going to shut down Central Expressway completely, dig it out and put six lanes on the bottom and they're talking about eight lanes on top and a light-rail system down the middle. . . . "

(For the record, DART officials say the freeway will never be completely shut down, will not be double-decked, will have eight lanes plus service roads and will have rail lines along each side.)

At SMU, Ronnie said the Mustangs are "one of the best football teams in the nation. They did not lose a single football game for the last three years in a row. There was a reason: They didn't play football."

(For the record, the Mustangs are not one of the best football teams in the nation. They lost nine games last year. They did not, however, play the two previous years.)

And while we're at it, here are just a few more things for the record: That sculpture on the SMU campus is The Mouse, by Claes Oldenberg, not Mickey Mouse Sad, and it wasn't donated by Walt Disney World; a plane never flew through that hole in the Texas Commerce Tower; Southland Corp. is not trying to sell all its 7-Eleven stores in order to build the second City-place Tower; Amtrak has three trains per day in Dallas, not two a week, and you don't have to wave your ticket to flag down the trains.

A Gray Line official in Dallas said guides are free to develop their own tour commentaries. But he said a review of those commentaries might be in order.

And for the record, the Gray Line tour did provide an extremely accurate and vivid portrayal of a Dallas summer. Midway through the excursion, the bus air conditioner broke down.

August 19, 1990

Remember when?
This woman does

OLD-TIMERS like me can remember when there was a department store in Dallas called Sanger's.

Real old-timers remember when the store was known as Sanger Brothers.

And then there's Willie Littlepage, who remembers the Sanger brothers themselves.

"Oh, yes, one of those Sanger brothers used to peddle out of a suitcase," she said. "He came to our house. Mama bought some material from him and made me a dress."

Old-timers like me moved to Dallas in the 1970s. Real old-timers came here in the 1930s and '40s. And then there's Mrs. Littlepage, who moved to Dallas in 1895.

In a covered wagon no less.

"Papa had a big woodyard, and one day he just closed up everything and we set out to travel," said Mrs. Littlepage, who now lives at the Buckner Baptist Retirement Village in far East Dallas.

Her family lived near Waco at the time. And Mrs. Littlepage was just 5, so her memories of the journey are a random collection of childhood impressions.

(If you're trying to do the math, let me help. Mrs. Littlepage was born Sept. 5, 1890. She turned 102 last week.)

There is one thing she does remember distinctly about the move –and mentions often to this day. "I had gotten a pretty doll and a little doll buggy for Christmas that year, and Papa gave them away before we left. They didn't want to take them with us."

Mrs. Littlepage doesn't know where all the family traveled, but she does remember bouncing along the landscape in the covered wagon. "I stood up most of the time behind Papa," she said.

She particularly remembers crossing the Red River—a dramatic event in the days before bridges. "We crossed it twice," she said. "The second time someone had just drowned. The water was high. Papa crossed first to see if the wagon could make it. Then he came back and got us. I just shut my eyes when we started down that big hill."

Of course, Mrs. Littlepage can't imagine why any of this would be of any interest to anyone. "Are you gonna put all that junk in the newspaper?" she asked me.

Apparently Mrs. Littlepage—Willie Stanley, then—was something of a feisty girl. And she remains feisty today. She was the oldest of her parents' 14 children. "They didn't know when to stop," she said.

And there's one thing she's still peeved about after 102 years. "First girl, and they named me Willie! Of all things, Willie! I can't believe Mama named me that when all the other girls had pretty names.

"I always said, 'My first girl, I'm going to name her Mary.' But she never did come along."

Mrs. Littlepage and her husband, Hugh, had two boys. Only her younger son survives. He's 80 and in very poor health in a nursing home.

When Mrs. Littlepage and her family first arrived in Dallas back in 1895, they camped out along the Trinity River, along with many other families.

Soon, her father opened a grocery across from the Old Red Courthouse, and the family moved into a house at Ervay and Akard, across the street from the First Baptist Church.

"Law, I think I saw most every building in Dallas go up," she said.

"The streetcars were pulled by mules and ponies then. The streets were dirt, and oh, it was muddy when it rained. To think how they have straightened it all out now!"

And she certainly saw those Sanger brothers do well for themselves, going from peddler's suitcases to a fancy department store.
"Oh, they had a big place," she said. "They had a funny staircase you could just step on right here and it rolled you right to the top. Then you could go around and ride it right back to the bottom."

An escalator, of course.

But it still worries Mrs. Littlepage that I might be foolish enough to print any of this. "They'll fire you from that paper if you put all this in there," she warned.

Well, Mrs. Littlepage, for you, I'm gonna risk it.

September 11, 1992

Tragic death inspired
life of beloved pastor

I'M TELLLING YOU, you just never know what you're going to find in *The Baptist Standard.*

OK, admittedly, the little weekly magazine of Texas Southern Baptists isn't the *National Enquirer.* But a couple of issues ago, I came across a historical nugget that astounded me.

Did you know that a pastor of the First Baptist Church of Dallas once shot and killed the city's police chief?

Neither did I.

And you thought Baptists were dull.

I discovered this incident in an article in *The Standard* titled "The Sweet Fruit of Adversity." It was about famous people who overcame tragedy to accomplish great things.

And at the end of the article, it said: "Finally, to Baptists, the name George W. Truett is of hallowed memory. Called from a Waco church to become pastor of First Church, Dallas, Truett was nearly driven from the ministry by a tragic accident."

Everybody knows about the amazing 50-year reign of the Rev. W.A. Criswell at First Baptist. But the man who preceded him, the Rev. Truett, was even more widely revered in his day.

(My great uncle was George Truett Carr—one of many boys of his generation named for the famous preacher.)

The article in *The Baptist Standard* gave a frustratingly brief account of the incident that almost cut short his ministry. So I did a little additional research.

Mr. Truett was called to First Baptist in September of 1897 and was immediately popular with the influential congregation.

One member of that congregation was Capt. J.C. Arnold, the city's much-admired 17-year chief of police. In February of 1898, Capt. Arnold invited the young preacher to accompany him on a bird hunt in Johnson County.

Here's how Mr. Truett's biographer (and son-in-law), Powhatan W. James, tells the story in his 1939 book George W. Truett :

"They went by train to Cleburne, Texas, where they were joined by their mutual friend, Dr. George W. Baines, pastor of the First Baptist

Church of Cleburne; and the three went by horse and carriage to the hunting grounds.

"Late in the afternoon, they were returning to the place where they had left the conveyance. Capt. Arnold was walking along a path a few paces in front. Truett shifted his gun from one arm to the other and in so doing the trigger on the hammerless weapon was touched. A load of bird shot struck Chief Arnold in the calf of the leg.

"It was not a very bad wound, but almost instantly George Truett had a premonition that it would prove fatal . . . ."

And sure enough, Capt. Arnold's condition steadily worsened. He was transported back to Dallas by train the next morning, gravely ill. He died that evening.

"Chief Arnold Is Dead," said a bold headline in the Feb. 6, 1898, edition of *The Dallas Morning News*. "Rev. Mr. Truett Grief-Stricken."

By all accounts, Mr. Truett was nearly overwhelmed with grief. In fact, the next day's newspaper said: "All sorts of wild rumors were flying about yesterday concerning the condition of Rev. G.W. Truett. Last night it was stated on the streets that the reverend gentleman was dead. Later it was reported that he had lost his mind. The stories were without foundation."

Josephine Nash of Dallas knows the saga well. As the niece of the renowned preacher, she grew up hearing whispered retellings of the tragedy.

"Oh, it was just a terrible, terrible thing," she said. "Uncle George was just absolutely crushed. In fact, he wanted to give up the ministry completely. He finally prayed it through, but it haunted him all his life."

First Baptist's dynamic young preacher of just four months did soon return to the pulpit. But he returned with a profound new air of compassion and empathy for others.

"It was a turning point," said Alan Lefever, archivist and church historian at Southwestern Baptist Theological Seminary. "It changed his ministry and made him much more effective."

The Rev. George W. Truett would remain pastor of First Baptist for the next 47 years and become one of the most beloved preachers of the 20th century.

And Dallas history got one of its weirdest footnotes.

April 9, 1995

Church holds special place
in residents' hearts

I PARKED under a tree outside the church and took a seat among the wooden pews inside. I was finally acting upon years of curiosity.

The little church had been a jarring sight each time I passed.

In the midst of one of the busiest, glitziest, most heavily developed corridors in Dallas, the old stone church looks like it belongs on a country road in another century.

And, in fact, the church once did sit on a country road in another century.

It's just that the dusty road happened to be Preston Road, and things have changed a bit in the neighborhood since 1886.

Today, Jesus Revival Ministry occupies the church at the bustling corner of Preston and Spring Valley Road. Only about 15 people were on hand as the opening prayer was said. But when the organist ripped into some bluesy chords, the faithful handful belted forth with hand-clapping, heartfelt singing.

Other families came streaming in, and the singing grew louder. Soon, two fellows with guitars and amplifiers had set up next to the young man playing drums.

I wondered if the jubilation could be heard in the big homes backing up to the church or in the cars zipping by on Spring Valley.

Before the service, pastor John Williams had told me that people stop by fairly regularly to inquire about buying the prime piece of real estate. "But we just lease the property," he said, "and I don't think the owners are interested in selling."

The owner is Mount Pisgah Baptist Church, which held services in the property from 1886 until 1982, when it moved to larger facilities on Webb Chapel Road.

And no, they're not interested in selling. "The pioneers of the church, oh yes, are very sentimental about the old site," church historian Jesse Arnold told me.

Mount Pisgah Baptist Church was organized on the third Sunday in June 1864 by a group of slaves, Mr. Arnold said. They first met under a big elm tree not far from the Preston Road site.

A white minister, the Rev. Robert Fabius Butler, helped organize the church. "Now why do you suppose a white man was involved?" Mr.

Arnold asked. "See, this was during slavery," he answered. "And African-Americans could not meet up without a white face being there. It wasn't allowed."

After the Civil War, most of the slaves stayed put as sharecroppers, Mr. Arnold said. And according to church tradition, they bought the Preston Road property in 1886. Dallas County deed records show the deal was completed in 1888.

A crude frame structure was first built on the property. Families took turns bringing firewood to heat it in winter. A larger, white-frame church was built later. Then, in the 1940s, the present sanctuary of Jacksboro stone was completed.

Mr. Arnold began attending Mount Pisgah in 1937, when he was 8 years old. We stood in front of the old church one morning last week, and he reminisced. "On Sundays, they would sell homemade ice cream and hot dogs and bologna sandwiches right out here to raise money for the church," he said.

In Far North Dallas, it sometimes seems that nothing is older than yesterday. But memories and traditions run deep for Mr. Arnold and other blacks whose families settled there long ago.

Mr. Arnold lives in a beautiful home on McShann Road, just off Preston, on property that was once a sharecropper farm. "I picked cotton on this very land as a boy," he said.

And not too long before that, other blacks had lived in captivity in the area.

I wondered about those slaves who first gathered beneath that elm tree. I tried to imagine their astonishment if they could see the church's surroundings today. But when I looked up the origin of the name "Mount Pisgah," I began to think maybe they foresaw more than we might know.

Pisgah, I learned, was the mountain ridge that Moses climbed to look over into the promised land. Moses never got there, but his faith delivered his people to the land of milk and honey.

I'm not sure Far North Dallas exactly qualifies as the promised land. But maybe those founders had faith that better days were in sight.

March 17, 1996

Few words ring
as true as Crume's

WHEN OLDER readers are struggling to come up with a compliment, they will sometimes say to me, "Well, I guess you're the new Paul Crume."

I'm always honored by the comparison. But I don't pay much attention to it either.

There will never be another Paul Crume.

Less-tenured readers may not even recognize the name. Or they may know it only in connection with the angel column we reprint each Christmas.

And that's a sad state of affairs. Dallas was blessed to have had a gentle poet and scampish wit in its midst for almost 25 years. He shouldn't be forgotten—or reduced to a single column.

A Christmas gift I cherish is one my wife gave me 15 years ago. It's a collection of his columns called *The World of Paul Crume*.

I remembered reading his front-page Big D column in my youth. But I wasn't old enough or wise enough to really appreciate them until I began to read from the collection.

Paul started writing his column in 1952—the year I was born, incidentally. His last column appeared Nov. 13, 1975. Three days later, he died of cancer at 63.

"He really was a remarkable man," Marion Crume said last week. She still lives in the house she and Paul shared in northeast Dallas. Their son, Chris, now lives next door.

Mrs. Crume retired three years ago after 37 years at the Hockaday School, where she was a teacher and then principal of the lower school.

Once there was a time when every new person she met asked, "Oh, are you related to Paul?" That doesn't happen much anymore, she said. But she still senses the admiration many hold for him.

"It's an old-fashioned word, but he was a gentleman. And he was a gentle man ," she said.

Pointedly gentle, sometimes. "An extremist, as everybody knows, is anybody who disagrees with you," he once wrote in a wonderful column on politics and friendship.

By age and circumstance alone, there will never be another Paul Crume. He had one foot in frontier America and the other in the space age.

He was born in the Arkansas Ozarks—in a log cabin, no less. "Despite this promising start," he would say, "it's as close as I ever came to the presidency."

He could write of helping his mother "warsh and wrench" the clothes in a boiling washpot. He could tell tales of pet pigs and drenched horses, of asafetida and mustard plaster cures.

"The first time he told me those stories, I didn't believe him," Mrs. Crume said. "But his family really did maintain a frontier life long after it ended for most others."

When Paul was 6, his family moved to tiny Lariat, Texas, northwest of Lubbock. And there, side by side with cowboy culture, he began to absorb the book learning of several dedicated teachers. He went on to the University of Texas, graduating near the top of his class.

"He really was, in many, many ways, closer to a Renaissance man than people who were educated at Harvard but had no knowledge of this other, frontier world," Mrs. Crume said.

Only in *The World of Paul Crume* would you find commentary on the death of novelist E.M. Forster along with recollections of a boyhood trip from Arkansas to Colorado by covered wagon.

He once wrote, "The wild geese were stirring on the night I was born, and it is said that their honks were like a chorus of celebration. Ever since I have distrusted goose judgment. They just might celebrate anything on impulse."

The geese were right, of course.

Paul Crume understood the heart-rending sorrow that often is at the core of human experience. That's the genius of the angels column.

But right alongside that sadness, he could always see the mixture of human frailty and nobility that gives us cause for laughter and celebration.

When I read from Crume, I can't help feeling smaller as a columnist—but larger as a human being.

Once again, he will handle the official duties on Christmas Day. But in the meantime, Merry Christmas from a lesser successor.

December 22, 1996

Our city is easier
to like than to love

THIS IS PAINFUL to admit. But a startling realization came to me the other day:

I don't love Dallas.

Ow! It hurts to even say it. And if I were smarter, I probably wouldn't. People in my job are supposed to have a big, boundless love affair with the city. That's the movie version anyway.

I really like Dallas. Is that good enough?

And I do dearly love many, many of the people here.

But what is it that prevents me from having that button-busting kind of civic pride? The kind that makes you proud to tell folks where you're from.

Do you?

Why is it that I don't feel about Dallas the way I do about Texas?

I love Texas. For all its foibles and foolishness, I love Texas. I love being from Texas.

But I don't see many bumper stickers that say: "I (Heart) Dallas."

Now please, don't take this as the standard Dallas-bashing that goes on among the oh-so-smart, oh-so-bored set. They want everyone to know they're just marking time in Dallas until flitting off to New York or Seattle or Prague.

I expect I'll die in Dallas.

This is my home now. My kids were born here. I have a great job. Lori loves hers, too. Good friends. Good church. Family close by . . .

And maybe that's why it's painful to realize that the city itself plays almost no role in my happiness.

I do remember feeling one of those bursts of lucky-to-be-here love for the city. It was fleeting.

It happened just before the 1993 Cowboys Super Bowl parade. There was a genuine party atmosphere in the streets of downtown Dallas that day.

As the parade began, I found myself standing at the back of the crowd, next to a man of about my own age. He happened to be black.

"It doesn't look like we're going to see much," I commented.

He laughed and said, "It doesn't look like we're going to see anything." But we continued to stand there, enjoying the pretty day and the festive crowd.

We stood in silence awhile, and then the fellow said: "You know the amazing thing about this? It has really brought the city together."

"It sure has," I said. "And we needed something."

"We sure did," he said with a smile. And that was all our conversation.

Well, a few knuckleheads quickly turned that festive day into something ugly. But that moment of bliss stays with me.

For a few minutes that day, Dallas was a most lovable city.

For starters, we had a sports team that we could all take pride in. I won't dwell on that topic.

But other factors were even more important. For one, we had a gathering spot, a focal point. On that day, downtown Dallas was what it ought to be: the crossroads of the city, the place to gather from every corner.

We talk and talk about Town Lake and a revitalized downtown. And we talk and talk.

Maybe most of all, on that day we had a festive spirit. We stood ready to kick back and enjoy life. And on a workday!

You know, Dallas doesn't really have a single festival to call its own. The State Fair doesn't count. That's just another civic exhibition.

Oh, there are lots of nice little festivals for little slices and segments of the city. But we don't have even one big blowout for everyone to enjoy, where we can all rub shoulders and savor our city.

As I understand our history, old John Neely Bryan picked this spot because it was a good place to do business. And that's still our reason for being.

Doing business isn't a bad thing. It just leaves a big empty spot in the city where the soul is supposed to go.

It occurs to me that maybe what I'm feeling is, in fact, love for Dallas.

But it's that bittersweet side of love that parents feel when a grade-A kid brings home a C-grade report card.

I'm so disappointed. . . . You have so much potential. . . . You could do so much better.

Kind of hard to put that on a bumper sticker.

March 23, 1997

Test your city savvy, urban IQ

SO HOW MUCH do you really know about this place we call home?

Today we find out.

After exhaustive research, here's the Official Test of Dallas Civic Savvy.

Remember, there are no winners and losers here.

Just smarter and dumber.

OK, pencils ready? Eyes on your own paper, please. We begin:

1. Long before there was a Dallas, this was known as the "Three Forks" region. Name the forks of the Trinity River.

2. When we talk about Dallas, we usually mean Greater Dallas. All or parts of 30 cities are located in Dallas County. Eight have two-word names. How many of these can you list?

3. It's important to know your place in the world. If you headed east from Dallas across the Atlantic Ocean, where would you arrive?

4. We all know that John Neely Bryan started this city. But where did he end up?

5. Name two Dallas pro football teams, not counting the current one.

6. Emma Peek was the first to do it in Dallas—In 1920. What?

7. Forget Fort Worth. Dallas has western heritage, too. Both Doc Holliday and Frank James lived here during the late 1800s. What brought them to these parts, partner?

8. Dallas has had some memorable lawmen, too. Who is the current sheriff?

9. Dallas thrived on it and had none of it. What?

10. Name the two greatest inventions ever devised in Dallas.

OK, pencils down. Pass your paper to the citizen in front of you for grading.

1. Actually there are four forks. The Clear Fork joins the West Fork near downtown Fort Worth. The West Fork then flows through the mid-cities and meets the Elm Fork south of Texas Stadium. The East Fork joins the river southeast of Dallas in Kaufman County.

As a matter of plumbing perspective, Dallas drinks from the Trinity north of town and flushes into it south of town.

In dry spells, 95 percent of the river's flow south of Dallas is from sewer plants. Yet that water is cleaner than the city's rain runoff.

2. Highland Park and University Park are easy. Did you get Dallas' other island city—Cockrell Hill? Add Balch Springs, Cedar Hill, Farmers Branch, Glenn Heights and Grand Prairie.

3. Maybe you think of Europe as our neighbor to the east, but Dallas shares its latitude with North Africa. Head east from Dallas and you land in Morocco, somewhere between Casablanca and Marrakech.

Feeling more exotic, aren't you?

And sorry, kids, but you can't dig straight through to China. You'll make a soggy arrival in the Indian Ocean.

4. The founder of Dallas died in the State Lunatic Asylum in Austin. And this was without ever driving LBJ.

5. The Dallas Texans and the Dallas Texans. The first Texans became the Baltimore Colts in 1953. The second Texans turned into the Kansas City Chiefs in 1963.

6. On Nov. 2, 1920, Emma Peek became the first woman in Dallas County to vote. It was 34 years later, in 1954, when a woman first sat on a jury in Dallas County. The first all-female jury was in 1957. It sentenced Alvin Peterson to 50 years in prison for marijuana possession.

7. Doc Holliday worked as a dentist in Dallas in the 1870s before moving to Arizona for a brief career in gambling. After brother Jesse was gunned down in 1882, Frank James worked here briefly as a sales clerk at Sanger Bros. Department Store.

8. OK, not all lawmen are memorable. Jim Bowles is the sheriff of Dallas County. Tarrant County would probably trade.

9. Dallas has long been famous for oil—and never produced a drop. But you never know . . . . The county's first gas well was drilled in Coppell two years ago.

10. Authorities agree that two Dallas inventions tie for greatness: In 1958, Jack Kilby of Texas Instruments invented the integrated circuit. In 1971, Mariano Martinez of Mariano's Mexican Cuisine invented the frozen margarita.

God bless Dallas.

December 6, 1998

What would King say?
It's time to reflect

I TOOK A stroll one afternoon last week along Martin Luther King Jr. Boulevard. It seemed a fitting way to observe the holiday.

And I asked a simple question of people along the way: If Dr. King could come back and look around today, what would he say?

Melvin White sat outside the MLK Center in South Dallas, enjoying the sunshine while waiting for someone inside. "He'd be happy," said 72-year-old Mr. White. "We still need to come together and cooperate more with one another. But I believe he'd be happy."

A young man was coming out of the center. "I think he would generally be satisfied," Tommy Bozeman said. "There is progress."

He gave me a grin and said, "We can certainly drink out of the same water fountain now." And isn't that a vivid reminder of how far we had to come?

Mr. Bozeman added: "In any society or group, there are going to be different opinions. Not just between groups, but within groups or races as well."

And that sure proved true over the next two hours of my walk. It proved true in the next two minutes, in fact.

"I believe he would be very disappointed," said Harlene Smith, sitting in the front office of Ben Howard Plumbing Co. "Disappointed in all the window dressing, in all the surface attention to problems that haven't really been addressed."

But what about the progress? "There's not enough to rejoice about," Ms. Smith said. "Where's the rejoicing when you look at all these vacant lots around here, where houses used to stand and families used to stay? On the other hand, we have a whole lot more jails and penitentiaries."

At the Square Deal Barber Shop, Vernor Kennedy sat up in the shine chair by the front window of his shop, watching the world from that perch.

"I've seen a bit," 82-year-old Mr. Kennedy said. And he believes Dr. King would be only partially pleased. "We've seen some progress compared to what I came through. But there's still some ways to go."

In a lot of ways, MLK Boulevard symbolizes the good news-bad news nature of the civil rights movement.

At one end, near Fair Park, the boulevard is bright and vibrant with new businesses—a Minyard supermarket, Bank One, State Farm Service Center.

At the other end, where MLK meets the Trinity River, progress is mocked by a cluster of liquor stores, filthy vacant lots and ghostly, wandering people.

Halfway in between, a carwash was bustling on this sunny afternoon. People and cars were everywhere. Music played and a party atmosphere prevailed. And if Dr. King could have been there?

"He'd be happy to see what he accomplished," Roderick Board said. "He made a whole lot of difference for a whole lot of people."

Mr. Board is 25 and operates his own business, Rod's Wrecker Service. "That's one of the things he accomplished right there," he said.

But across the parking lot, 28-year-old Alvin Williams was wiping off his Mustang convertible and seeing things a whole lot differently. "He'd be disappointed," he said.

Why? "Just look around," he said. "He had a dream, but this ain't it."

In the middle of the boulevard, a man sold Nation of Islam newspapers. He wouldn't give his name but gladly answered the question: "He'd be mad as hell. He wouldn't be happy just because a street is named for him when one street over you've got all kinds of prostitution and dope and crack."

So what's the solution? Again, more disagreement. At Cultural Insights bookstore, owner Damond Fields said nothing will change until whites truly apologize and make amends for 300 years of brutal oppression.

At Jeff's Jewelry & Swap Shop, owner Jeff Aycock said: "Right now, y'all aren't the problem - white people, I mean. We're our own worst enemy."

So if racial issues seem strained and confused today, well, it's no less so along Martin Luther King Jr. Boulevard.

But as I walked, out of those different views, I began to hear the voice of Dr. King and what he might say to us today.

Take joy in our progress—without falling into complacency. Draw passion from our problems—without falling into bitterness or despair.

January 18, 1998

Kid Stuff

THESE ARE the columns that are most precious to me now—the ones about my kids. These are now like old faded snapshots of Allison and Corey as they grew up. There are sweet moments and some painful chapters here that even I had forgotten until I went back and reread them.

There's sort of a newsroom ethic that says you shouldn't write about your kids. So I tried not to too often. But the family columns were always among the favorites of many readers. And it's certainly not that my kids were all that fascinating. These columns simply reminded every parent of their own children and the adventures involved.

One of the questions that I have gotten most often over the years is: "What do your kids think about being in your columns?" And I think I'm fortunate that I could truthfully answer, "Nearly nothing." I guess they were young enough when I started that it has simply been no big deal to them. And I always tried to respect their privacy by asking permission before writing about them in a column—even one here about a certain undergarment.

So thank you, Allison and Corey, for being good sports, for being the joy of my life—and for providing so much good column fodder.

The play's the thing
in girls' softball

I ATTENDED my daughter's first softball game last week.

It had all the finesse of a train wreck, but she sure looked cute in that uniform.

And though she got to bat only once, I think she showed a lot of natural flair for the game.

Just before she stepped to the plate, the coach put his arm around her and whispered a little batting tip: Don't swing at anything.

(He had detected a hint of wildness in the opposing pitcher. Most pitches were hitting the dirt. A few hit the umpire.)

So my 10-year-old softball prodigy stepped into the batter's box and did nothing. Flawlessly.

In fact, she was still standing motionless when the umpire politely informed her that he had called four balls and she was invited to proceed to first base at her earliest possible convenience.

She seemed pleased.

I don't want to say that our team is inept, but it appeared that the Angels had mastered only one softball skill—chatter.

Like a plague of ponytailed locusts, they buzzed incessantly while in the field.

"Heeeyy, batter, batter, batter, SWING!" they cried with every pitch.

But they were soon demoralized when the other team took the field and seized the upper hand with rhyming chatter:

"Hey, batter, what's the matter? Can't you stand a little chatter?"

The girls in our dugout tried to recoup with some extemporaneous return chatter.

"We've got the pitcher and the catcher all shook up," they chanted.

But of course that effort fell flat. It neither rhymed nor scanned, and they soon gave it up.

Still, I think our team has shown tremendous potential in this area.

Only a few days earlier during a practice, the whole outfield suddenly broke into a heartfelt singing of "Lost In Your Eyes," a hit song by fourth-grade fave Debbie Gibson.

The coach seemed a little unsure of how to handle an outbreak of Top 40 music in the outfield, so he relied on the old baseball standby. "Hey! Heads up out there!" he yelled.

In the early innings of this first real game, our team relied primarily on the Mathematical Defense. Like the Cowboys' famous Flex Defense, the Mathematical Defense is rather complicated, but I will attempt to explain it: When the other team scores five runs, it's your turn to bat again.

This rule is intended to hurry games along and avoid the midnight curfew in most city parks.

Despite the shaky start, our girls remained in good spirits.

I don't want to dwell on the differences in boys' and girls' baseball, but having watched my son play several seasons of baseball before giving it up for soccer, I can't help but see subtle differences.

Intensity, for one. These girls seemed dangerously close to confusing competitive sports with fun.

I have never seen a boy skip in from the outfield.

When boys step into the on-deck circle to await their turn at bat, they stand with their backs to the spectators, taking ferocious swings of the bat with studied concentration. They would rather die than acknowledge old Mom and Dad sitting in the stands 5 feet away.

Girls, on the other hand, seem to regard the on-deck circle as a little theater in the round. They take bat in hand, adjust their caps, step into the circle and immediately turn to the stands to flash brilliant smiles.

Their eyes roam the crowd, making sure that they command the full attention of parents, grandparents and cute older brothers of teammates.

I must admit that parents also behave differently at these games. I can honestly say that in all the time my son was playing baseball, the Team Mom never issued me a miniature cowbell painted in team colors with a fluffy bow to ring on the boys' behalf.

But in the important things, there are no differences.

The Angels battled back in the game to lose by only a single point, showing a lot of courage and competitive spirit.

When the game was over, they met in the dugout to analyze the outcome, to frankly assess their strengths and weaknesses.

And like the most veteran softball players, they came to an honest conclusion: "The umpire was unfair."

April 26, 1989

So much for youth's sweet innocence

AH, THE innocence of youth!

I wonder what ever became of it.

It seems children now fall into three stages of development: infants, toddlers and short adults.

Last weekend my 10-year-old daughter and her mother went shopping. I must be careful in the telling of this tale, lest Allison never forgive me.

Suffice to say that, after weeks of contemplating the deed, Ali purchased her first upper torso undergarment. She returned home positively giddy with equal excitement and embarrassment.

I was genuinely moved by this milestone in her life. "This is a historic day," I said, playing the sappy father to perfection. "I can't believe my little girl has grown up and has her first . . . (upper torso undergarment)."

"Yep," she said. "An over-the-shoulder boulder holder."

Thud.

That was the sound of my jaw hitting the floor—quickly followed by the crashing sound of a shattered sweet moment.

"Where in the world did you hear that?" I asked, my voice reaching for the upper octaves of indignation.

I had only recently heard the phrase for the first time myself. It's in the lyrics of a crude, campy Bette Midler song on the "Beaches" soundtrack. I couldn't imagine that Allison had also heard it there.

"Punky Brewster," she answered blithely.

For those not wise to pre-teen culture, Punky Brewster is the lead character in a television show by the same name. She's a girl about Allison's age.

Ali went through a phase of not just watching Punky Brewster but worshiping her. She repeatedly asked for permission to legally change her name to Punky.

I pointed out that Punky Blow didn't have the same ring.

I had always assumed that television was responsible for early-onset worldliness in children, but I never suspected that Punky Brewster was in on the plot.

A month or so ago the kids were playing with their cousins, working hard to create some sort of ambitious business enterprise.

"We're going to give all the money we make to the homeless," cousin Zach said.

I praised them effusively. "That's really sweet," I said.

"We figured that's the easiest way to get on the TV news," Zach said.

Media manipulation at age 11. Not a pretty sight.

Allison was just 8 or 9 when I was educated to the extent of her education. In the car, she began massaging my shoulders, and I moaned with pleasure. Abruptly she slapped the back of my head. "You sound like the people in that movie," she scolded.

Unfortunately, I knew instantly what she meant. The night before we had watched a movie with an off-camera romantic scene. No nudity. Just sound effects. I was certain that it had gone over Allison's head.

"Maybe she was massaging his shoulders," I said. A lame effort, I'll admit.

Allison slapped me again. "Here's a hint: They were in the bedroom with the door closed," she said.

"So?" I said.

"Second hint: they weren't wearing any clothes."

I was committed now. "So?"

"Third and final hint," she said. "They were doing what you have to do to make a baby."

"Oh," I said, trying to sound like a calm, modern, we-can-talk-openly parent. "They were making love."

"Right," Allison said. "Sex."

Well, I knew there was one father-daughter talk we needn't have.

Honest, I'm a good parent. I don't let the kids watch R-rated movies. It must be the neighborhood kids spreading this wisdom.

My son Corey just turned 9, but he's been enthralled with the sound of the word "sex" for a long time.

Awhile back, in a burst of sweet talk, he told one of his school girlfriends, "I'm gonna sex you."

Fortunately, this suave overture was not reported to the authorities.

One day I finally asked Corey exactly what sex is.

He didn't hesitate. "It's when a man and a woman take a bath together and then jump into bed—without even drying off!"

Ah, the innocence of a very limited number of youth.

May 17, 1989

A kid's values can
throw his dad for a loop

AS A SON gets older, it gets harder for a father to express his love.

A son grows embarrassed by kisses long before a dad does. And eventually a son won't sit still for hugs.

So that just leaves World Class Championship Wrestling.

Now suppose someone asked me to name the absolute last place I would like to be on a fine Friday evening.

The immediate answer: "12-Man Thunderdome Anything-Goes Tag-Team Wrestling."

And yet, when the opening bell clanged Friday night at the "world-famous Sportatorium," guess who was sitting in the fourth row. Hint: ages 37 and 9.

How do I love thee, Corey? Let me count the ways: Kerry Von Erich vs. Tarras Bulba, Gorgeous Gary Young vs. Flamboyant Eric Embry, Jimmy-Jack Funk vs. Al "The Latin Heartthrob' Perez, and on and on.

Corey knows I don't really approve of wrestling and its silly manufactured mayhem. We go through a little ritual each time I find him glued to a televised wrestling match.

"Corey," I say, as a wrestler performs a flying knee drop on an opponent's skull, "is wrestling real or fake?"

"It's fake."

"Are those people really hurting each other?"

"No."

"Are you ever going to try any of that stuff on your sister?"

"Yes."

"Corey?"

"No."

"OK. Enjoy it."

Then I go on about my business, feeling that I am only a bad parent, not a terrible one.

Unfortunately, when Corey heard about this 12-man Thunderdome deal, he felt he had to see it in person. So did a lot of other people. The scenic corner of Cadiz and Industrial was swarming. We paid $2 for the privilege of parking behind a liquor store, then hiked to the arena.

Corey was enthralled with the preliminary matches. He was thrilled to see his favorite, Gentleman Chris Adams. And it was clear that

Mr. Adams is indeed a gentleman. Only twice did he pick up a chair and threaten to bash his opponent.

Flushed with the excitement of seeing good triumph over evil, Corey said at one point, "When I grow up, I want to be a wrestler."

I tried hard to find some socially redeeming value in all this commotion. I tried looking at it as a form of dance—full-contact choreography.

Nah. . . . No matter how hard I tried, it still looked like grown men wrestling in their underwear.

Finally came the main event. A chain-link fence was erected around the ring—the "steel-cage Thunderdome." The wrestlers climbed inside, and the orgy of violence really began. Within minutes, blood was flowing down the faces of almost all 12 wrestlers.

I remembered seeing on a news program how wrestlers sometimes use tiny blades to cut themselves on the forehead, which causes dramatic bleeding but little danger.

I don't know if that's what these guys were doing, but they all seemed to sustain identical forehead injuries.

It was a sickening spectacle of blood and sweat and bad acting.

"Let's go," Corey said suddenly, before the event was fully over.

"Really?" I asked. "Yeah, let's beat the traffic," he said.

So, as the 12-man Thunderdome lunacy wound to a close, we headed for the car. "That was gross," Corey said. "If they ever show that on television, I'm going to turn it off."

"I agree," I said, trying not to sound pleased. "Do you still want to be a wrestler?"

"No."

"Why not?"

"What I saw."

A smart kid.

We drove home talking of other things. But as we neared the house, he returned to the subject. "Do you know what I really want to do when I grow up?"

"What?"

"I want to go around to different sporting events and charge $2 for parking."

A very smart kid.

August 16, 1989

Supply-side fight
puts Dad in school daze

I NEVER went to Vietnam, but I was in Wal-Mart on Monday night.

It's not something I like to talk about. But, yes, I was part of the Back-To-School Death March.

This was part of the grisly offensive known as The First Night After The First Day Of School. If you've got kids, you were probably there, too.

Our unit had engaged in many other back-to-school shopping skirmishes over the past few weeks. I felt certain that our job was done.

On Sunday night, back-to-school eve, we had spread all the supplies out on the floor for sorting and inspection. We were equipping two kids. It looked like enough for a small Appalachian school district.

Back when I was a kid—yes, there's that phrase you swore you'd never use back when you were a kid—school supplies were a more modest undertaking. In crayons, the 48-count box was the most you could hope for.

Now it's an inalienable right of every child to get the 64-crayon, double-wide box with built-in sharpener—though no one in the history of the world has ever successfully sharpened a crayon.

No child can reach full potential these days without benefit of crayon colors such as mahogany, aquamarine, bittersweet and periwinkle.

I was pleased, however, to see that the crayon color called "flesh' when I was in school has now been renamed "peach." Corporate Crayon America finally realized that much of this nation is mahogany.

As we sat in the floor Sunday night, Corey proudly demonstrated the latest in notebook technology—the $2.1 billion stealth notebook named the Trapper Keeper.

Trapper Keepers are decorated in outlandish colors and carry names like Street Hawg or Rude Dog or Insensitive Cow.

They come with Velcro flaps, hidden pockets, clipboard springs and many other classroom disruption devices.

So off to school the kids went Monday morning, loaded down like pack mules. And home they came Monday afternoon with the list of school supplies they would really need (as opposed to the official list of school supplies posted just for laughs in all the stores).

It's at this stage of the game that kids come home accusing you of betraying them by sending them to school with two-hole, college-ruled notebook paper. With trembling lips, they say they will be expelled from school and turned over to juvenile authorities if they don't have three-hole, wide-ruled notebook paper BY TOMORROW!

This year, Corey also came home with a list of supplies his teacher doesn't allow.

Trapper Keepers, for one. And I hadn't even made the first payment.

By now, Allison had also checked out what all the other girls brought to school in the way of supplies, so she had her own official list of socially imperative school supplies needed BY TOMORROW!

First on her list was a scented school supplies box. I doubted the existence of such a thing.

So Monday night, we embarked on a final shopping assault. It was a Wal-To-Wal-Mart nightmare. The checkout lines extended beyond the batteries and National Enquirers all the way across the front aisle and into the plastic storage bowls.

As an initial strategy, I tried humor. "Hey, let's come back when there are more people," I said. Allison gave me one of those "dads are so-o stupid" looks.

Unfortunately, you can't swat a kid just for rolling her eyes. Not in public anyway.

So I fell back to Strategy No. 2: The Dad-stands-off-to-the-side-and-looks-impatient routine. The kids elbowed their way into the school supplies trenches. Allison returned periodically to hold scented supply boxes up to my nose.

Finally, it was time for Strategy No. 3: Wade in and bark orders. Corey, keep the GI Joe lunch box, but put the toy football back. Allison, save the scented-supply-box search for another day—and preferably another parent.

Exhausted, we staggered home. The kids fell into bed without even remembering to protest the new "totally unfair' back-to-school bedtime rules.

I was tired, but the back-to-school war was not quite won. I plopped into the floor for hand-to-hand combat with book covers, which had to be on BY TOMORROW!

August 30, 1989

Midsummer night
whips up magic

IT WAS nearing midnight, and I was savoring the last few pages of a book when Allison came into the bedroom with a crisis.

"There are two June bugs buzzing around my room," she said. "They are keeping us awake."

Allison's best friend, Kristina, was spending the night. I suspected that had more to do with their being awake than the June bugs.

I finished my book and walked down the hall to Ali's room. As luck would have it, one of the offending June bugs was waddling down the hall toward me. Sometimes life is good.

I scooped up the beast and bounded into the girls' room, making a big, hammy entrance. "When the bugs are bad, who ya gonna call? Bug Busters," I sang, displaying my capture.

They laughed like I was a comic genius. Silly 11-year-olds make such a wonderful audience.

I went to the front door to pitch the bug out and noticed that the wind was really gusting. I walked out into the darkness to investigate. A storm was skirting to the south. Lightning flashed in the distance, and the wind felt hot and dry.

Suddenly feeling frisky, I ran around to Allison's bedroom window and pounded on it. Then I scurried back inside and walked nonchalantly to her room.

The girls were chatting just as nonchalantly. We talked a few minutes. Finally I was forced to ask, "Did you hear anything?"

"No. Where?" Ali responded innocently. She looked at Kristina, and they howled with laughter. They had beaten me at my own game. Savvy 11-year-olds make such a rotten audience.

"You scared us to death," Ali finally conceded. "Come outside," I said. "It's neat."

The girls happily followed me out, wearing their cartoon-character nightgowns. They stood in the driveway a moment and then went crazy—running and jumping and giggling, intoxicated by the warm night, the eerie wind and the late hour.

The girls began to dance in the driveway. "Watch a cute boy come by," Ali said, half fearful, half wishful.

Then, in an act of wild bravado, she turned around, flipped up the tail of her nightgown and shook her white-cottoned bottom at the world.

Kristina broke up in hysterical laughter. She's a good friend that way.

"Ooooh," the girls gasped. The lightning off to the south was putting on a spectacular show. "It lit up that cloud," Kristina said.

I pointed out a bright star over the neighbors' roof. "That must be the evening star," I said in an authoritative voice.

Then we noticed that the evening star was moving rapidly to the west, apparently cleared for landing at D/FW. Oops.

"I see a puppy," Kristina said. She was pointing to the clouds overhead. We strained to see more shapes. "I see a porch light," Ali said. She was pointing to the house across the street. More laughter.

The wind really began to howl. Ali grabbed me, as if she might blow away. "I'm Dorothy," she said. "This is Kansas."

Kristina said something about the wind direction, and both girls held up pointer fingers, as if to test the wind. "You have to lick it," I said, popping my index finger into my mouth. They did likewise. "Now, which side feels cool?" I asked. "That's the direction the wind is coming from."

The girls were impressed. My mouth tasted like a dirty finger.

The wind gusted even stronger. A garbage can down the street blew over with a loud, creepy clang. Allison held her fingertips to her forehead, as if getting a vision. "I'm psychic," she said. "I predict that tonight I'll be sleeping in your bed."

Some prediction. She's been doing it every stormy night for 11 years.

She and Kristina ran inside. I lingered awhile, reluctant to let the night go.

You know, as modern families, we work hard at having a good time—rushing here and there with the kids, spending loads of money on this and that. And then, suddenly, you have more fun than you can remember in months, all because of a warm, windy, giddy summer night.

I went back into the quiet house and walked down the hall to Ali's room to check on the girls. I switched off the lamp shining in their sleeping faces.

July 25, 1990

Kids are blue over
lack of fashion jeans

THE WORLD agonizes over the Persian Gulf Crisis.

The nation wrangles through the Great Budget Debate.

And at my house, we wrestle with the Cavaricci Question.

Forget war and taxes, we're talking really important stuff here. We're talking school clothes.

If you haven't heard, Z. Cavariccis are the latest thing in britches. And here's the best part: They cost $75 a pair.

Here's the worst part: Both my kids are dying for a pair.

Now, ordinarily, this wouldn't be a difficult issue. I'd give the kids a thoughtful answer. "$75?" I'd say. "Ha!"

But I'm afraid it all raises some painful memories from my own adolescence. Yes, friends, I was a victim of socially incorrect blue jeans. Unlike Corey and Allison—fifth- and sixth-graders—I don't recall even being aware of fashion as a grade-school kid. We were all equally poor at Mattie Jones Elementary.

But then I hit junior high school, got mixed in with some of the richest kids in town and quickly learned the terror of fashion.

In hallways full of Levis, I was the dork in the J.C. Penney jeans. As I recall, they were called "Foremost" jeans. And no matter how many times you washed them, they stayed stiff, starchy and bright blue.

How I coveted that little red tag on all those Levis.

But my dad, bless his frugal accountant's heart, didn't see any reason to pay $9 for a pair of Levis when perfectly good Penney's jeans could be had for $4.50. With reinforced knees!

I have forgiven Dad, of course, but the memory remains. And now my own children come to me, saying, "Dad, can we get just one pair of Cavariccis?"

And I hear myself say, in my own father's voice, "That's outrageous. We're not going to spend $75 on jeans."

"But so-and-so has a pair," they say, "and they're poorer than we are."

"Maybe that's why they're poorer," I retort, trying to remember if that was another line Dad used.

"Daaa-yud," they plead. And I feel trapped between prosperity and common sense.

Through the grade-school grapevine, I heard of a place in Garland that sells Cavariccis at a discount. Out of curiosity, I stopped by Linda's Fashions. A sign near the door immediately caught my eye. "Cavariccis. Reg $75. Only $59.99," it said.

Oh, "only" $60.

"Your kids must be young," owner Linda Ainsworth said. "Cavariccis have been hot in the high schools for a couple of years, but now they are really hitting the middle schools and elementary schools."

Admittedly, Cavariccis are pretty neat-looking. You could almost describe them as zoot suit pants, but then no kid would know what you're talking about.

In 12 years of specializing in school clothes, Mrs. Ainsworth has learned just how cruel a combination fashion and children can be. "One mother came in here almost in tears. She was a single mother with four kids. She said the other kids at school were throwing pennies at her kids because they didn't wear the right clothes. We made a special price for her."

But Mrs. Ainsworth said fathers can be pretty obstinate about the price of Cavariccis. "Mothers understand what things cost these days. But these dads come in here, and they haven't shopped in years, and they don't wear anything but Dickey jeans from Kmart. They can be hard to deal with."

In defense of those hardhearted fathers, however, we might be right.

"That's a tough one, but don't give in," counseled child development specialist Susan Wyatt of the Dallas Association for Parent Education.

"I know it's hard on their ego, and they think they're going to die. But any excesses are really harmful for children," Dr. Wyatt said. "You've got to set reasonable limits for children and explain why those limits exist. It helps them become responsible adults."

At our house, we have forged a compromise. I've told the kids I'll pay half the price of a pair of Cavariccis if they can earn the rest.

I think they're planning a garage sale with their grandmother.

Now, if only Congress and Saddam Hussein could be so reasonable.

October 17, 1990

Kids' absence puts you at a huge loss

WHEN WE began drawing plans for a new house a few years ago, we had two children approaching adolescence.

And so, as we pondered the things that we could and could not afford in the new house, one of our priorities became bathrooms for each of the kids.

It meant giving up on some things Lori and I really wanted. But trying to force a teen-age boy and a teen-age girl to perform their hair-combing rituals in a shared bathroom seemed like a formula for disaster.

Better that Iraq and Kuwait should share a bathroom than Corey and Allison.

So now they each have their own bright, fully equipped bathrooms. And guess what?

They use ours.

On most mornings—despite two empty bathrooms upstairs—our dressing area looks like backstage at the circus.

There is jostling for mirror space. Allison's contact lens paraphernalia mixes with my shaving gear. And nobody can ever find anything.

"Where's the hairbrush?" "Who used the nail clippers last?" And "What happened to the backs of these earrings?" (Corey and I stay out of that one.)

These flare-ups invariably end with my saying, in exasperation, "Why don't you kids use your own bathrooms?"

But do you know what? The other morning I was dressing after everyone else had left, and I was suddenly overwhelmed by the silence of that bathroom.

It occurred to me that in just a very few years, I'll be wistfully recalling those mornings when we fought for mirror space.

Why is it that we appreciate our children most in their absence? You know what I mean. When they are underfoot, kids can drive you crazy. But let one of them go off to camp or grandma's for a few days and you miss them like crazy.

That morning, in my moment of melancholy, I think I had just a glimpse of the enormous emptiness that must follow the loss of a child.

It made me want to rush right up to school, dash into my children's classrooms and hug them. (For which I would never be forgiven, of course.)

I recalled a poignant story I had read months before.

Randolph Severson is director of counseling for Hope Cottage adoption center. In his book, *Adoption—Charms and Rituals for Healing*, Dr. Severson tells this story:

"My lesson came from an older man who didn't know enough to use the word 'infertility.' He hadn't been educated, as we say.

"After seeing each other in therapy for a few months, he ended a session by asking me if we could skip a week since the next week he had something he had to do.

"When I asked him what, he explained, in a rather matter-of-fact voice, that next week's session fell on a day that 20 years ago he and his wife had lost their baby.

"It was a boy, and he had been stillborn. And they had never been able to have any other children.

" 'So, every year on that day, I go fishing,' he said, 'so that up there, in the stillness, with the water lapping quietly up aside my boat, I think of all the things that me and Bob—we named him Bob—could have done together.

" 'You know, it has been so long, it's got down to three things I think on.

" 'I wanted to show him how to ride a bicycle. I wanted to run along behind him with one hand on the seat and the other on the handlebars and then see him take off and go with me standing there smiling.

" 'I wanted to take him to a baseball game and smell that sweet spring night air, and watch somebody steal second base. I wanted him to see a good, fast, smart runner crouch and go, a whirl of white going lickety-split down that line, then slide cleats up and see that umpire holler 'safe.'

" 'I wanted to sit out one summer evening, a good blanket under our butts, but one that you could feel the grass underneath, and I wanted to show him the stars and name them the way my daddy did me. 'Orion's belt.' 'Orion's belt.' I wanted to say those words to him.

" 'And I do say them out loud, with just me and the old fish listening . . . .' "

January 27, 1993

Life with teens like scenes in a horror flick

I WAS SEATED at a luncheon the other day with a group of older ladies. We were all making small talk around the table, getting to know each other a little.

And then I said something that brought the conversation to a momentary halt.

When I said it, the woman seated next to me shuddered visibly.

There were a few gasps and some knowing nods around the table. One woman shook her head and said, "I'll pray for you."

This was my startling confession: "I'm now the father of two teen-agers."

See, you flinched, too.

When was it that we became scared of our own kids?

This is really not fair. I spent my childhood in mortal fear of my parents. Now I'm spending my adulthood in mortal fear of my children.

I feel like if I make one wrong move as a parent, my kids will end up on a street corner in Deep Ellum with purple hair, spikes in their noses and sub-par SAT scores.

I don't know why I'm burdening you with this. I guess I just need a little support.

Corey turned 13 the other day. Allison is 14. And I feel like I'm standing on the edge of a cliff.

No, that's not really true. It's worse than that. Now that Corey has become a teen-ager, too, I feel like Evel Kneivel strapped to a motorcycle and racing toward a leap across a bottomless canyon— Troubled Teen Canyon.

Will we make it across? Will we crash and burn? Is there any way to just park and get off?

All these years I thought those jokes about teen-agers were just jokes. But they really DON'T clean their rooms.

And explain this to me. Over dinner, I can't get two words out of moody Miss Allison: "Fine," "Yes," "No," "OK."

Then she goes to her room and jabbers on the phone nonstop for four hours.

I really thought that was just a joke about teen-age girls on the telephone. It's more like a part-time job.

Silly me, I always assumed that *The Exorcist* was a horror movie. Now I realize that it's the true story of a normal adolescent girl.

One minute she's perfectly sweet. The next thing you know, her head is spinning and she is growling at you in a voice you've never heard before.

I guess that's the disconcerting thing about all of this: Just as you get used to having these little kids around the house, they suddenly turn into full-size people you don't know.

I'm startled sometimes to see this long, lanky young woman who now lives in our house.

And Corey appears to be on the verge of growing into his feet.

Actually, I have to say that I'm very, very proud of my kids so far. Allison was elected "Miss Sunnyvale" at her junior high this year. Of course, it's a very small junior high. But I'm proud nonetheless.

Corey got his share of honors, too. He was named "Most Improved Player" on the seventh-grade basketball team.

I have to admit, however, he had a big advantage over the other boys. He takes after his dad, which means he had enormous room for improvement.

In my determination to keep Corey and Allison on the right path, I pushed them into taking volunteer jobs this summer at a senior citizens center near our house. They were OK about that, but I crossed the line when I suggested they ride their bicycles to the center.

"What is this?" Allison snarled (with a hint of a smile). "Something out of the 1950s? Riding our bikes to the old folks' home!"

I hadn't thought about it in just that way, but, yeah, I guess I would like to find a way to raise my kids in the 1950s. Or maybe the 1890s.

But unfortunately, here we are in the 1990s, headed for that wonderful adventure called The Teen Years. I have no idea what path the journey will take, but I do know how I would like it to end.

It occurred to me a few years ago that my own parents had begun to seem less like parents and more like wonderful friends—a couple of fellow grown-ups I'm lucky to know.

When my own family gets to the other side of this Troubled Teen Canyon, I hope to find a couple of friends waiting there.

June 6, 1993

Seeing a child off to college:
The Waco wail

I DON'T WANT to get into that old game of parental one-upmanship.

But don't come to me with your sad stories of little first-graders heading off to school, lunch boxes in hand.

And don't tell me about your nervous ninth-grader starting high school, backpack slung over one shoulder.

If you want to talk about the depths of parental despair, let me tell you about sending a child off to college—with moving boxes!

If you thought you heard civil-defense sirens last weekend, that was just the wail of my wife on the way home from Waco.

Me, I was just fine. That enormous lump in my throat kept me from making a peep.

Oh, I know, I know. Some of you are rolling your eyes. It's not the end of the world. It's not that big a deal, you say.

It's also not your kid missing from that empty, empty bedroom down the hall.

Yes, we took Allison off to school Saturday for the start of her college career—and the end of her childhood.

Oops, there's that siren again.

If we're going to get weepy here, we might as well go all the way. How does anyone survive the loss of a child? What unfathomable sorrow.

We only lost ours to Collins Hall at Baylor University. And we're a mess.

Maybe this is God's way of helping parents forget the pain of tuition.

This whole college separation thing is new for us. Lori and I had a different sort of sorrow attached to our college career. We were married.

So when dorm move-in day came on Saturday, we were just as wide-eyed as Allison. We arrived at Baylor with our own little caravan—Ali's car, my minivan and Corey's truck, all loaded down with the bare necessities of dorm life.

I really wanted to tie boxes on the roof and write "Baylor or Bust" on the windows, but Ali was looking for a more discreet arrival on campus.

So our nondescript little caravan fell right in with the traffic jam of similarly loaded vehicles arriving on campus.

Have you ever watched an ant hill?

That's what Collins Hall looked like Saturday morning. Streams of little worker ants pouring in and out of the mound, dodging each other while struggling under huge loads.

Mini-refrigerators. Rolls of carpet. Computers. Bookcases. Crates of hair-care products. Did I mention that Collins Hall is a girls' dorm?

Over at the boys' dorms, it was a different story. Guys arrived with TVs and garbage bags stuffed with clothes.

The clothes went straight in the corner, and the guys spent the rest of the day trying to get better TV reception.

Meanwhile, back in Collins, mothers were carefully putting up matching window treatments and wallpaper border.

Lori felt like a real failure as a mother. We arrived without border.

The important thing is that Ali got a great roommate. Jennifer Nelson is from Amarillo and seems very sweet. That's a good thing, because it's going to be very cozy in that dorm room.

It was like a jigsaw puzzle, but we finally got all the furniture arranged in the room. Jennifer can work at her desk without getting out of bed. And Ali can sit at her desk and brush her teeth at the sink at the same time. They have to take turns standing up.

Oh, it's not quite that bad. But it will be like living in a hotel room for a year—a budget hotel. The bathrooms are down the hall.

All in all, things went well Saturday. At least until the end.

In one of the freshman-orientation sessions, they actually told us how to say goodbye. Do it in the dorm room, they said, not out on the curb.

Well, Allison and Lori were both blubbering like crazy when the moment came. Jennifer was there, and they got her crying, too. I was just trying to keep a quivery chin steady.

We all exchanged hugs, and Lori and I turned quickly to walk out. We hadn't gone but a few steps down the hall when we heard Ali let out a huge, heart-piercing sob.

Somehow we managed to keep walking. But it was on wobbly knees.

You know, I have never been a fan of home schooling. But I'm starting to like the idea of home colleging.

August 27, 1997

Kids' leaving fills
house with silence

LISTEN.

Hear that?

The silence, I mean.

That's the sound of an empty nest. Creepy, isn't it?

About this time last year, as you might remember, I was dealing with the "Waco wail."

That was the civil-defense-siren sobs of my wife and daughter as we left Allison behind for her first year at Baylor University.

Well, this year we made the move all over again with our son. Our last. And Lori and I are facing something far worse than the Waco wail.

It's the Sunnyvale silence.

It's the eerie hush that has settled on our house since the kids departed one week ago.

I'm telling you, I have never felt so discombobulated. A house without kids? I can't fathom such a thing.

No blaring television? No ringing phone? No shoes in the middle of the floor or friends traipsing through? No mess in the kitchen?

It's horrible, I say.

I might get used to it, but right now it's horrible.

Remember back in the '60s when we first started sending folks into space, and we were all so amazed by the concept of weightlessness. That's how I feel—weightless.

Lori and I drift around the house, feeling sort of lost. We sit listlessly at the kitchen table, and it seems as if the spoon might just float right up out of my hand.

We've lost our center.

Oh, I know, I know. Those of you with kids in their Terrible Twos (or Sevens or Fourteens), you're thinking how wonderful a few moments of peace would be.

Well, trust me. The day will come. And I hope you're better prepared for it than we were.

Somewhere in these last 20 years of child-rearing, I think we forgot to have a life.

Are parents allowed one?

Just the move was weird enough. I can't tell you how anticlimactic it is to move a son to college compared with the grand procession of installing a daughter in a dorm room.

Last year, it was as if we were Egyptian slaves, moving the Queen of Sheba into Collins Hall. The process went on for hours.

This year, we carried Corey's few boxes into Penland Hall, he kicked them into the closet, and we were done.

Ba-da-bing. Ba-da-boom. Get outta my room.

We retreated across campus to Allison's new apartment, where major nesting was going on.

We had moved her in the day before, along with three roommates. But that was only the beginning of actually settling in. Twenty-four hours later, hair-care products were still being sorted, stacked and arranged.

At one point, while work continued in the bedrooms upstairs, I took a break and stood for a quiet moment at the dining room windows. And the thought struck me: "I'm looking out the windows of my daughter's apartment."

My daughter's apartment!

Those words just don't compute. My daughter's bicycle. My daughter's playhouse. Those are words that make sense to me.

But here we are. Or I guess I should say, there they are.

I know I should be excited. This is a turning point, a time to do something different with my life. Let's see, I could join a fitness center, start graduate school, date an intern . . . .

So far, I've replaced the kitchen faucet.

Somebody once told me that nature has a way of easing the pain of the empty nest. They said that teenagers are so obnoxious that when they're finally gone, you're glad.

And I remember that phase. But in our case, it's a classic example of bad timing. Because here's our experience:

Just when they become people you like, they leave.

August 30, 1998

Heroes

THESE WERE the hardest columns to select. I simply had too many. I've had the privilege of writing about far more heroes than I could possibly fit into a single chapter.

To me, a hero isn't a professional football player or someone on the cover of People magazine. A hero is simply someone who displays courage or unselfishness—often in the smallest, quietest ways.

So meet Kris Robinson and Jimmy Daniels and little Shon Tate. And remember that they represent the many others that I had to leave out. Remember, too, that all the people I have written about represent only the tiniest fraction of courageous, unselfish heroes working quietly in our midst.

A child speaks
to Grandma about faith

JUNE ARNOLD began putting out her Christmas decorations last week. Ordinarily, that would be nothing special. Her mammoth Christmas decorating job has always started in October.

For the last 20 years, June and David Arnold's spectacularly decorated home on Midway Road just north of Northwest Highway has been a Christmas landmark.

June is such a Christmas nut, in fact, that one room in her home stays decorated for Christmas all year long.

But this was the year June thought she wouldn't celebrate Christmas. "I just didn't have the heart,' she said. "I thought there wasn't a Santa Claus anymore, I was so sad and disappointed."

Then, a few days ago, her grandson asked her to put up a Christmas tree. And that was something special.

It is almost a miracle, in fact, that 6-year-old James LoMonaco is able to ask aloud for anything.

James was born profoundly deaf. Doctors told his parents, John and Pam LoMonaco, that he would never hear or speak.

But the doctors didn't know Pam, a woman of extraordinary optimism, with beauty to match. Pam, June's daughter, began talking to experts all over the country.

At the same time, another Dallas mother was conducting a similar search. Laurie Spitz's daughter also was born deaf. The two mothers met at a support group for parents of hearing-impaired children, and they quickly became allies in the search for alternatives to sign language.

Their search eventually led them to an audiologist in Denver whose work with new hearing-aid technology and speech-therapy techniques was enabling profoundly deaf children to hear and speak.

Gradually, Pam and Laurie's mission to help their own children broadened to include all hearing-impaired children in Dallas. And they worked together to open a non-profit program here.

But even as Pam worked to establish The TALK Center for Hearing-Impaired Children, she was beginning to fight her own health problems. She suffered excruciating headaches. And in July of last year, doctors told Pam she had a brain tumor.

Surgery was performed a few months later. But as June said, "It was hopeless from the start. The surgery revealed that it was malignant and widespread."

Though Pam was confined to bed much of the following months, she remained an undaunted worker for The TALK Center. "We talked on the phone every day," Laurie said. "Pam was the real visionary. She was always bubbly and smiling."

The TALK Center opened in February, and it was an instant success. "We boomed," said Linda Daniel, the new director. The center, temporarily located at Shearith Israel synagogue, opened with nine children. It serves 25 today.

"I think each child should have a chance to learn to talk, a chance to live in our world—the hearing world," Laurie said.

Even as The TALK Center flourished, however, Pam's health declined.

Ultimately, June slept beside her 36-year-old daughter every night. "I worried what I should do when the end came," June said.

On the morning of Friday, Oct. 5, June was singing to her daughter and stroking her hair. "When she breathed her last, I just kept singing to her," June said. "I didn't do anything else. To have tried to wake her up would have been a sin."

Even in death, Pam contributed to the future of The TALK Center. There is a new zeal now, Laurie said. And numerous memorial donations have strengthened the center's finances.

As death neared, Pam worried that her little boy would not remember her. But June doesn't worry. "When he's a grown man and realizes what she did for him, how could he forget her? She allowed him to live in the hearing world."

More than that, Pam will have helped scores of other children enter the hearing world. "Through her perseverance, doors have been permanently opened to children who may never know her name," a friend wrote in tribute to Pam.

"But every time one of those children rejoices in life, he or she will echo Pam's spirit. Generations from now, lives will stilled be touched by Pam LoMonaco."

And this year, the Christmas lights will continue to shine.

October 28, 1990

Ex-addict shares
his good fortune

I HEARD THE name and figured I could guess the story.

The Ethel Daniels Foundation operates non-profit alcohol and drug treatment programs in the city. Rich old woman, I figured. North Dallas, probably. Died and left a load of money for a good cause. Hooray. End of story.

Little did I know.

Jimmy Daniels interrupted himself as we talked and pointed outside the garden windows of his East Dallas home.

"Do you want to know the most ironic thing about me?" he laughed, pointing to the security sign in his flower bed. "I have a burglar alarm system now. They used to put those in to keep me out."

Jimmy, 48, had just run through the early highlights of his life in a kind of shorthand form.

"Grew up in a housing project in Louisville, Kentucky," he said. "In a fatherless home. Mom raised all of us kids on welfare. There were 10 of us.

"Quit school at 16. Married at 18. In the penitentiary by my early 20s."

Then he backed up for a most significant point. "Also by the time I was in my late teens, I was a full-blown drug addict and alcoholic."

He went to prison the first time for forging a federal check. "While I was in prison, my wife was murdered," he said. "And man, that's when I really just gave up."

His second trip to prison was for burglary.

His third was for armed robbery.

And his fourth was "just for being a drunk." He had gotten four DWIs in 22 days.

Jimmy then drifted to Dallas. One of his brothers was living here—a brother he was close to. "We were in prison together."

Jimmy worked off and on in dental laboratories around town. At 15, he had worked as a delivery boy for a dental lab back home and had learned a little of the trade. He had been faking it ever since.

But mostly he drank. Jimmy was in and out of the Dallas County jail on various drug and alcohol charges.

Then, finally, he hit bottom.

"I had lost my job. I had lost my girlfriend. I had lost my apartment. I was sleeping in my car," he said.

It embarrasses him a little now to tell it, but Jimmy hatched a cockeyed plan to get himself back on his feet. He would find a woman to take him in, he thought. And he would find this woman by jogging around the apartments off Upper Greenville Avenue.

In an alcohol haze, Jimmy began to run. But he stumbled and fell. And there, face down in an empty field, he began to cry.

"I just started cursing God: 'You killed my wife. You never gave me a father.' I even cursed him for making me ugly."

And in those moments, something happened. "I don't really understand it. I've had people tell me that I surrendered."

He found his way to a fellowship of recovering alcoholics—people unashamed to admit their own weakness and to trust in a higher power for help.

"I found God's people, and it changed my life," he said.

When he had been sober for five days, Jimmy found a dentist willing to use his services, and he started his own dental laboratory.

When he had been sober for five years, Jimmy took $50,000 from his successful dental business and started a halfway house for other recovering addicts and alcoholics.

And he named it the Ethel Daniels Foundation—not for a rich old Dallas woman, as I had guessed. He named it for his wife, the young woman murdered 16 years before while he was a drunk and a drug addict serving one of four prison sentences.

Today, four years later, the Ethel Daniels Foundation operates on a half-million-dollar annual budget. It is one of the most respected programs in town.

Daniels Dental Studio now does work for 25 dentists. And Jimmy Daniels, approaching nine years of sobriety, counts himself one of the most fortunate people on Earth.

We're all a little cynical now. People don't change, we say. This whole notion of resurrection seems a little hard to buy—even in the midst of spring, even on an Easter Sunday morning.

But not for Jimmy Daniels. He knows the power of resurrection. "I have been redeemed, liberated, transformed and set free," says he.

March 31, 1991

STEVE BLOW   **49**

Adversity takes two men
down different roads

WITHIN A MATTER of days, I heard from two different people offering similar column ideas.

Each wanted to know more about someone they pass along the road each day. Two men beside the road—one a source of inspiration, one a source of irritation.

I stopped first by a construction site along Strait Lane in North Dallas. An empty wheelchair stood in the midst of the heavy machinery.

"He's working down in the hole," a worker explained.

He told me that Gary Ray—the wheelchair's owner—operates a tunneling machine 30 feet below the surface, 12 hours a day.

The best time to catch him, he said, would be during the lunch hour. And so I promised to return.

The other man, on the other hand, was right where the caller had said he would be. He looked to be in his early 30s, a burly fellow with thick curly hair and a bushy beard.

He stood along the North Central Expressway service road at Lemmon Avenue, holding a scrap of cardboard.

"I Want Work—I Am Hungry," said the crude lettering on his sign.

He looked most unhappy when I walked up and introduced myself. "I don't want anything in the newspapers," he said.

Lots of people read the newspaper, I said, and one of them might have a job for him.

"Nah," he said.

Clearly, he wished I would go away.

He wouldn't tell me his name or much about himself. Was he really hungry? "Yeah," he said without conviction.

And what sort of work was he looking for? "I'm on disability," he said.

So, was he really looking for work? "Sort of," he said.

Finally, I asked the real question: Was he standing on the street corner in hopes of a job or a handout?

He didn't answer that one at all. He just stared at me until he got his wish. I went away.

The next day I went back to the construction site and caught up with Gary. He and his buddies were dusting off and heading for lunch at a nearby cafeteria. I tagged along.

Gary, 26, lives in Fort Worth. He's soft-spoken but straightforward. He isn't bothered that people are curious about him, he said.

"Ross Perot stopped by the other day. He lives near there," Gary said. "He just said he admired me for working."

It was five years ago that Gary lost both his legs just below the hips. He was working for the same construction company then—Southland Contracting Co. Driving home at the end of a long day, he fell asleep.

"I flipped the truck over a couple of times and got tangled up in it. It landed on top of me," he said matter-of-factly. "They didn't find me for a couple of hours. I was down in a creek bottom."

He was conscious the whole time. "It was very painful."

Gary was out of work for three years—but not by his choosing.

"I liked to went crazy those three years I sat around the house. I wanted to work," he said. Finally, after some other jobs fell through, the construction company offered to give him a try again. No one was sure what he could do—if anything.

He began as a crane operator. But soon it was clear that Gary was ideally suited for the cramped, grueling work of operating the tunneling machine. "It's easier to get around in there without legs," he said.

Gary spends his days inside a tunnel 4 feet in diameter, boring a new sewer line through solid limestone. "When you're 1,200 feet up in a tunnel and look back and can't see daylight, it gets a little eerie. But it doesn't bother me," he said.

Gary isn't one for poetic statements on overcoming handicaps or beating adversity or any of that mumbo jumbo.

It's just a matter of economics and happiness.

"Sitting around the house with no money gets real boring. The government will pay you enough to survive on—but not enough to really live on," he said.

"The way I feel about it, I'd rather be working and have a little money to spend."

Two men beside the road. One of them with a tragic handicap.

June 9, 1991

Teen comes to terms
with regurgitation

WARNING: If you have a delicate stomach, please do not read this column.

But if you love truly sick, adolescent humor, please read on.

WARNING: If you find stories about cancer just too depressing, then stop now.

But if stories about courage lift you up, please continue.

Christopher Garrett was a senior at Dallas" arts magnet high school last year when he began to notice a shortness of breath.

"We all have asthma," said Chris' mother, Elizabeth. "We just figured it was that."

It was not.

Chris, 19, was diagnosed as having a particularly virulent form of cancer. On Valentine's Day, he began chemotherapy.

Though debilitated by both the illness and the treatment, Chris kept going. An accomplished violinist, he pursued his music studies at the arts magnet and managed to graduate with his class.

"It was difficult, but he walked across the stage at McFarlin Auditorium," Mrs. Garrett said. "He was very thin and very bald, but he made it across."

Despite his illness, Chris also finished his few remaining requirements to become an Eagle Scout. With special permission from Boy Scout headquarters, the presentation ceremony was in Chris' room at St. Paul Hospital.

And then there was another little project that Chris pursued. (WARNING: Sick humor ahead.)

For more than a year, the chemotherapy kept Chris violently nauseated. More to the point, he was throwing up constantly.

Somewhere in the midst of this misery, Chris and his friend Ignacio "Iggy" Gallegos began compiling a list of all the many terms for that unpleasant act.

They came up with 108, including a few inventions.

The list was posted in Chris' hospital room, and nurses got involved in the project. They're experts in the field. Eventually, doctors, too, were stopping by to add their favorite euphemism.

Soon, psychotherapist Clare Chaney learned of Chris' list and was using it with other cancer patients to show the value of humor as therapy. It was Dr. Chaney who told me about the list.

I went to see Chris last week at St. Paul. He was very sick. It was an effort for him just to talk. And yet a spark of wit still gleamed when he talked about his words.

"I've grown quite fond of them," he said.

And so, without further ado (and with only a few delicate deletions), here is the list:

Throw up, upchuck, barf, puke, Ralph, yack, glurt, yark up, hurl, spew, keck, retch, sparf, choof, Buick, gob, gag, purge, heave, Yugo, yarf, boot, gorge, chug, spout, throttle, chortle, turtle, lose your lunch, toss your beans, blow your cookies, blow doughnuts, blow groceries, blow lunch, blow cheese, blow beets, liquid laugh, technicolor yawn, intestinal souffle, lunch launch, power boot, sludge swimming, whistling beef, chuck chicken, lunch revisited, power belch, Mardi gras, bile bawl, call Earl, bile backstroke, refried meal, tequila turnover, Bacardi belch, spleen nuke, spleen splash, liver loogie, Total Recall, McYac to go, license to spill, hydrochloric tea-time, mozzarella mouth missile, digestive deja vu, hail the general, sing Yankee Doodle, call John on the big white phone, deliver a street pizza, ride the stone pony, take the bus downtown, play poker with Cindy, worship the porcelain god, and involuntary personal protein spill.

Chris' favorite: the almost polite-sounding "choof."

Even Mom liked the list. "It has helped us laugh through some terrible situations," she said.

Yesterday morning, as I was writing this column, Dr. Chaney called to let me know that Chris had died during the night.

"It wasn't expected so soon," she said. "But he and his mother had a great heart-to-heart talk last night. He was ready."

And she said the family very much hoped that I would go ahead with this column.

"In a wonderful, warped sort of way," Dr. Chaney, "it would be a great tribute to Chris."

And so shall it be.

March 6, 1992

Love letters bring war
to heart, mind

WHEN WORLD WAR II came along, young Orvill Raines was just making his mark as a cub reporter at *The Dallas Morning News.*

With hard work, Orvill had gone from errand boy at radio station WFAA to obit clerk at *The News* to full-fledged reporter.

But the war called, and he went to the South Pacific aboard the destroyer Howorth.

Orvill did not stop writing, however. He wrote letters almost daily to his beloved wife, Ray Ellen. They were long, heartfelt missives full of love and loneliness, with vivid descriptions of both the tedium and terror of war.

Earlier this year, those letters were published by Westview Press in a powerful book called *Good Night Officially.*

The title comes from a little joke between Orvill and Ray Ellen. As newlyweds, they had trouble ending their bedtime conversations, even after repeatedly saying "good night." So they adopted the rule that when either said "good night officially," no more conversation was allowed.

And throughout the war, they continued to silently tell each other "good night officially" at bedtime each night.

The book's editor, historian William M. McBride, said Orvill's letters provide one of the most vivid accounts to emerge from the war.

In some letters, Orvill simply longs for home. "The guys in the Torpedo Shack have the nicest map. And the nice thing about it is: It has DALLAS set right down there in Texas where it oughta be. It's really silly I know, but I can look at that map and see Dallas there. Then I visualize the city itself and you darling. I say to myself that you are right there. Not so far away . . . ."

At times, he could be painful in his honesty: "I am like a lost child without you Ray Ellen. Can you imagine a little 2-year-old kid lost in the Christmas crowd . . . too bewildered even to cry? That's your full grown husband, Darling."

As the war dragged on, Orvill worried about his career. "I will be pretty well left out of things as far as the newspaper is concerned," he fretted.

But then, with touching innocence, he vowed to become the best reporter on the paper. "I promise you right now that when I walk into the city room at *The News*, the copy boys and reporters will turn to visitors and newcomers and say, `That's Raines, the red-hottest reporter on the staff.' "

Though usually upbeat, Orvill couldn't help facing the possibility of death. "We are taking men to their doom. As sure as the screws are churning us through the water, the men riding the ships I watch day after day are going to their death."

And he saw many die in the bloody battle for Iwo Jima. "I sincerely pray to God that the people of America will not forget the sons who died there. It was the Devil's own creation."

By March of 1945, Orvill was headed for Okinawa and writing freely of his fears. "Okinawa spells Kamikaze Corps to us."

On April 6, he dashed off one of his shortest letters. "Just a line. I have to hurry . . .," he wrote. "Bye darling, more later."

A few hours afterward, at 5:08 p.m., a Japanese suicide plane slammed into the bridge of the Howorth. Orvill was thrown overboard, badly burned. And he died there in the sea, in the arms of a shipmate.

Sadly, Ray Ellen did not live to see the book. The Garland woman died last December, just weeks before its publication.

She had remarried, and husband Guy Dewey said he takes pride on her behalf in both Orvill and the book.

Orvill proved to be a good reporter to the end. He had arranged for a final letter to be delivered in the event of his death: "My Darling Baby Ray Ellen," it began, "I hope that you never read this . . ."

He went on to express his love for her and his thoughts on meeting death. ". . . Remember that my last breath was drawn in an effort to get back to you. That my last thought was of you and if I cried, it wasn't from pain of wound but pain of not holding you in my arms again.

"All the love, devotion and worship that any man can give a woman I give to you in this, my last 'Good Bye Officially.' "

August 21, 1994

Family's lives changed
in tragic instant

THERE'S A phrase Allen Short uses often these days: "In the blink of an eye."

"Everything can change," he says, "in the blink of an eye."

One moment, Allen and his family were cruising along LBJ Freeway in the family van. "We were singing along with the radio," he said, "just being silly."

And then came the blink.

"I didn't even realize what had happened," he said. "I felt this big bang, and we jolted forward. I looked in the rearview mirror, and all I saw was flames."

What had happened is that a 19-year-old man, driving fast and allegedly drunk, slammed into the back of the family's van. Brandan Waddell is charged with intoxication assault.

The van went spinning out of control. "When we finally came to a stop, I started yelling: 'Get out. We're on fire. Get out. We're on fire,' " Allen said. "But when I looked back at my family, they were all unconscious."

It was the evening of Aug. 3. The Shorts were passing through Dallas on the way from their home in Wichita Falls to see relatives in Alabama.

Allen had to kick his door open. Then he pushed his wife, Debbie, out her passenger door.

When he turned to rescue their two teenagers, the back seat of the van was engulfed in flames. That's where his 17-year-old stepson, Kris Robinson, was trapped.

The flames were beginning to reach the middle seat, where Kris' 14-year-old sister, Kelli, was regaining consciousness.

"She started screaming," Allen said. "But just as I reached for her, people came up and pulled me back. I didn't realize it, but I was on fire—my ball cap and my shirt."

He jerked away and returned to the van. With the help of a passer-by, he pulled Kelli out.

But for Kris, there was nothing they could do.

"It was a nightmare," Allen said. "The worst nightmare."

A fire truck happened to be passing by. It stopped and doused the flames. Only that piece of luck saved Kris' life.

Allen was treated and released that night for minor burns on his head and back. Debbie spent three days in the hospital for burns on her arms, legs and face.

Kelli was burned over 25 percent of her body. Her left arm was broken, and she underwent an operation to stop internal bleeding. After more than two months of daily therapy, she finally started classes at Wichita Falls High School two weeks ago.

But for Kris, a long struggle remains.

He was burned over 70 percent of his body. His neck was broken, leaving him paralyzed. His spleen was removed in emergency surgery.

"Doctors told us not to expect him to live through that first night," Allen said. "Here we are 89 days later, and the doctors still don't know if he will survive. But they are getting more and more optimistic, just like we are."

He remains in intensive care in Parkland Memorial Hospital's burn unit. The few areas of his body not burned are now raw from skin grafts. Surgeons have sewn his eyes shut in hopes of saving them from infection. Someone must place a speech device next to the breathing tube in his throat so he can talk.

And yet, somehow, Kris remains upbeat. "He's determined. He's very determined," Debbie said. "He's not quitting."

Allen and Debbie have been living at Ronald McDonald House since the accident. Their day revolves around the four 15-minute visits allowed with Kris.

They said his spirits—and theirs—have been sustained by a flood of support from classmates and the whole community of Wichita Falls, where Allen is in the Air Force.

But this is a week when Kris could use even more support, they said. He turns 18 on Friday.

If you would like to send a birthday card or a note of encouragement, mail it to Kris Robinson in care of Ronald McDonald House, 5641 Medical Center Drive, Dallas, Texas 75235.

"He's a great guy," Debbie said.

"He didn't deserve to have everything taken away," Allen said, "in the blink of an eye."

November 1, 1995

Burned youth turns 18, aided by gifts of love

AGAINST ALL ODDS, it was a happy birthday.

Kris Robinson turned 18 Friday in what surely must be the world's worst place to celebrate a birthday—the burn unit at Parkland Memorial Hospital.

But thanks to a combination of Kris' courage and an incredible outpouring of support from many of you, it was indeed a happy day.

I told you about Kris and his family in a column last Wednesday. The Wichita Falls family was passing through Dallas on vacation Aug. 3 when their van was struck from behind and burst into flames.

The other driver, 19-year-old Brandan Waddell, is awaiting trial on intoxication assault charges.

Tuesday afternoon, I caught up with Kris' parents, Allen and Debbie Short, outside the burn unit on Parkland's sixth floor. Nurses were about to wheel Kris to surgery for yet another skin graft operation.

"Wait here with us. You can see Kris," Debbie told me. "Be prepared," she warned. "It's a gruesome sight. But it's so much better than it was."

Soon Kris' hospital bed was wheeled into the hallway. I won't belabor Debbie's description. "Gruesome" is the word.

Kris was burned over 70 percent of his body, including his face and head. His eyes are sewn shut to save them from infection.

"Come to Mama," Debbie called out as Kris was wheeled toward us. As he passed by, she teased, "Hey, where's my smile?"

Kris' lips are burned back from his teeth in a perpetual ghostly smile. But at his mother's voice, the lips widened into the real thing. "There it is. There's my smile," Debbie cooed.

"I love you, Son," Allen called out as Kris was rolled into a waiting elevator.

Then Allen and Debbie began their usual wait. This was the 12th such surgery for Kris. And while they waited, they talked about an extraordinary birthday.

"I really thought his birthday was going to be horrible for him," Allen said. "I'm so glad I was very, very wrong."

What made the day special, they said, was an incredible display of compassion and concern from across the city. Allen estimates that 7,000 cards and letters were received.

Mail arrived by the basketload at their apartment at the Ronald McDonald House. Handmade cards came from schoolchildren across the area. Almost 100 helium balloons were delivered. And then came flowers and fruit baskets.

"When we got back from our noon visit on his birthday, outside our door there were mounds—and I mean mounds—of letters, cards and packages," Allen said. "And it kept coming all day long! It was just unbelievable."

That day, for the first time since the accident, Kris sat up in a chair. And Debbie read to him from the cards.

"I said to him, 'These people don't even know you. But they know that what happened wasn't fair. And they're pulling for you. They're praying for you.' He just shook his head. It meant so much to him."

One of the most touching letters began: "Dear Kris, My name is John and I am writing you this letter on behalf of the firefighters at Dallas Station 43. My fire engine was first on the scene the night you and your family were involved in the accident. After that night, we never thought that we would have the opportunity to speak to you through this letter. Your life was changed forever that night and so were ours. We think about you all of the time and wonder how you're doing. Sometimes we call the nurses to check up on you.

"We are very sorry that this tragedy had to happen, but you could not be in better hands. The people at the Parkland Hospital burn unit are the best in the world.

"When you get better, please let us know how things are going. We wish you the best of luck and a speedy recovery. You will always be in our prayers."

The letter was signed by Lt. John Ostroski. And there was a P.S.: "I hear today is your birthday. Happy Birthday!! My son Matthew was born on November 3rd also. Tonight, when we sing happy birthday to Matt, we will light another candle for you too. Take care."

A lot of candles have been lit for Kris Robinson in hearts across this city. And his family is forever grateful.

November 8, 1995

Burned teen finds
there's a lot to live for

THE INTERVIEW began with the usual pleasantries. But little else was routine.

I typed the words "Hi, Kris" on a keyboard. The letters appeared on a large, lighted message board right in front of Kris Robinson.

"Hello," he said.

"How are you?" I typed. He studied the words, then in labored, halting speech, replied, "I am doing better than I was—much better than I was."

I first wrote about Kris back in November. He was about to celebrate his 18th birthday in intensive care at Parkland Memorial Hospital's burn unit. Almost 20,000 of you sent birthday greetings and later messages of support.

Kris was burned over 70 percent of his body last August when an allegedly drunken driver slammed into the rear of his family's van on LBJ Freeway. For months, he was semiconscious, a heartbeat from death.

He remains hospitalized, now at Healthsouth Medical Center in Dallas. He is paralyzed from the shoulders down. He is deaf. He has faint vision in only one eye. His facial features were largely burned away.

So, putting pleasantries aside, I asked him how he's really doing.

"I'm far from being 100 percent," he told me. "But at least now I can function. I'm completely alert all the time. I'm eating. I'm very well. I'm recovering."

I asked him if he realizes that thousands of people across the city are pulling for him. "Oh, goodness yes," he said. "When they told me how much mail I had gotten, it just blew my mind. There are a lot of good people out there."

I confessed to Kris that I feared he would not survive. "A lot of people didn't think I would make it," he said. "The doctors put me in a drug-induced coma to die peacefully. But I came out of it.

"When I woke up, I couldn't hear. Couldn't see. Didn't know where I was. A little frightened. But I came through. The Lord is merciful."

I typed, "Amen!" And Kris laughed.

A couple of months ago, Kris suddenly awoke, fully aware and alert. Using a message board and sign language, he has been studying with a teacher from the Irving school district. This week, he will complete the requirements for his high school diploma.

And what then? "My father says I have to take a year off," he said. "I don't want to, but I think I will—to learn sign language real well and to see how well I can recover from this. And then, college."

Kris said he doesn't remember the wreck. He has only a vague impression of his mother speaking to him. "She says, 'Hang on. Sirens are coming. Do you hear them? They're coming.' I say, 'Mommy, I'm hurt.' Then I say, 'I hear them. I will hang on.' "

In the hospital room, stepfather Allen Short wiped back tears. "After 10 1/2 months, I still tear up," he apologized.

I asked Kris how he feels about the young man who hit their van. Brandan Carl Waddell, 20, remains charged with intoxication assault. He has since been sent to prison for violating probation on an earlier drug conviction.

"Well, I have mixed feelings about him," Kris said. "Part of me thinks he's scum. But the other part of me feels he's just a person who made bad choices."

Kris paused a long while, then said, "I do think I could forgive him."

The thought has occurred to me before that I wish I could march every teenager through Kris' hospital room, to contemplate the responsibilities of driving.

I asked Kris what he would say to people who drive too fast. "Well, I admit that I've got a heavy foot sometimes," he said. "But you have to think you're not just endangering yourself.

"Driving fast, that can be condoned," he said, sounding like any other teenage boy. "But driving inebriated, there's no excuse for it."

I congratulated Kris on his courage. "Thank you," he said. "I found out there's a lot to live for."

Is he ever scared? "It depends. Am I scared to die? No," he said. "For a short time, I had no hearing or vision. That was nightmarish. But I'm not scared of dying. I'm not scared of living the rest of my life as a cripple."

I typed out, "You can be happy?"

And Kris replied, "I am happy."

June 16, 1996

Teacher hasn't been
a prisoner of circumstances

HER FATHER WAS a raging alcoholic. The desperately poor family moved from one dump to another. And when she was 10, her father finally carried out his threats.

He shot her mother to death right in front of all five children. And as they ran for their lives, he turned the gun on himself.

With no family to care for her, she was shipped off to a children's home. And you can probably guess the rest....

Right, she became a wonderful, happy, well-adjusted wife, mother and teacher.

Hmmm. Not what you expected?

We tend to believe these days that childhood cements our destiny. Jerre Simmons stands as a one-woman refutation of that theory.

This week, the beloved teacher at Duncanville High School will retire. "She is gracious, loving, supportive—all those things," said colleague Frances Phillips. "She doesn't know how wonderful she is."

"I call this my palindromatic moment," Mrs. Simmons joked. "I'm 63 years old, and I've been teaching 36 years. It's the perfect time to retire."

Palindromatic? Can you tell she's an English teacher?

As Mrs. Simmons tells her life story, it's hard to believe she's not reciting from some tragic Southern novel. "I was born in Honey Grove, Texas," she said. "My family had lost everything in the Depression. And I don't guess they had ever had very much.

"My father was a tenant farmer, and we moved a lot. My father was also an alcoholic. The very worst kind—the kind who took his pay, got drunk and then came home and abused his wife and children. He tried many, many times to kill my mother."

Mrs. Simmons was the oldest of the children. She remembers one drunken, murderous rage in particular. "My mother and I carried the babies and ran out into the cotton fields and hid. The cotton was high or he would have found us."

When the rage passed and they slunk back into the house, her father had smashed every dish and shredded every piece of clothing in the house.

Later the family moved to a two-room house in Dallas. She remembers that the children were washing their hair that day. 'He came in with a gun. My mother's last words were, 'Oh, John. No, no....' "

The children fled from the house. "As I ran, I heard another shot and remember thinking, 'She wasn't dead. He shot her again.' " It was the suicide shot.

I looked up the local newspapers from Aug. 5, 1943. Front page photos show five solemn-faced waifs. "Home Sought For Children After Slaying," said the *Times Herald* headline.

"I keep saying I'm going to write it all in a book one day," Mrs. Simmons said. "I already have the first line. I want to say: 'I grew up in a foreign country, just outside Dallas.' "

That was the Buckner Orphan's Home. "It was like its own country, with a fence around it," she said.

Mrs. Simmons has come to love the place only in retrospect. "We felt like we were just in a holding pattern, that life would really begin only when we graduated and became like everyone else."

We expect children to be permanently scarred by such trauma. How could Mrs. Simmons have emerged so whole?

"Well, I never have seen a counselor," she said with a laugh. "My people don't go to psychologists."

She certainly credits Buckner with providing safe haven. And she brags on husband Bill, "my rock," for 42 years of support.

But, fittingly, this celebrated English teacher says her primary salvation came through words. Just words.

She talks about the books that sent her imagination soaring from a lonely orphanage. She talks about the poetry of John Donne and Emily Dickinson that helped her fathom the human condition.

Most of all, she recalls the words of encouragement that people in her life provided at exactly the right moment. "It seems that at times when I faltered, there was always someone there," she said. "To me, it has always been words that have healed and comforted."

In her classroom, in her life, Mrs. Simmons has been a testament to the transcendent power of words. And now she's earned two of the sweetest: Happy retirement.

May 19, 1996

Child brings warmth
to Christmas

THIS IS THE story of a little boy who brought Christmas to his family.

Now, just by looking, you certainly wouldn't think that Shon Tate could provide Christmas for a whole family.

After all, he's only 6 years old.

Shon and his twin brother, Joshua, are first-graders in Plano's Aldridge Elementary School.

At Aldridge, they have a program called STOP. That stands for Students Thinking of Other People. And this year, they decided to have a holiday sock drive—to provide socks for emergency shelters around town.

In Shon's class, teacher Robin Keating would start each day by collecting socks. "We always made a big to-do when someone brought socks," Ms. Keating said.

On a cold, cold morning a few days back, several students came forward with socks. Shon was among them. And Ms. Keating was touched.

Shon is one of nine children in the big, extended family of Bernard and Sterlinia Tate. Most of the Tates' children are grown. Tragic circumstances prompted them to take Shon and his two brothers into their home. The Tates are the only mama and daddy they have ever known.

Mr. and Mrs. Tate are retired and have health problems. But caring for small boys keeps them going.

"They're just really a nice, nice family," Ms. Keating said. "The children always look so nice and are so well-mannered. And Mrs. Tate is up at the school helping whenever she can."

Ms. Keating didn't know the full circumstances of the family's finances. But as little Shon stepped forward with the socks that morning, the thought struck her that it was certainly a generous gift.

There was another passing thought as she took the socks—their temperature seemed a little odd. But Ms. Keating quickly went on with the busy details of getting a school day started.

It was a few hours later, as the students went to PE, that Ms. Keating realized what had happened. "Shon squatted down in front of me to tie his shoe, and I saw that he didn't have any socks on. And that's not at all the way his mother would send him to school," she said.

"And then it dawned on me: He had slipped his little socks off on the sly and handed them to me for the sock drive."

Now Ms. Keating was even more touched. She and her students had talked many times about helping those who are less fortunate. But she had never seen a student take clothes off his back—or socks off his feet—to help others.

She wrote a letter of praise to Mrs. Tate (and surreptitiously returned the socks, careful not to hurt Shon's feelings).

Over the next few days, Ms. Keating told friends about the generous act she had witnessed. They, in turn, told other friends. And before you know it, someone had sent the family $500. Another sent $150. And some sent lesser amounts.

When Mrs. Tate called to thank Ms. Keating for the gifts, she had a question. "Do you think it would be OK if we used some of it on utility bills?"

It turned out that the family had been without gas since summer. They've been heating bath water on the electric stove. And Mr. and Mrs. Tate have been fretting as they faced each new cold spell.

"I never ask nobody for nothing—except the good Lord upstairs," Mrs. Tate told me this week. "So when this came to us, I couldn't help but cry. God sure knew what we needed."

After the utility bills were paid, enough money was left over to buy a few toys for the children. But Mrs. Tate said that having the heat on is the very best gift of all—even for the kids. "You think they're not enjoying that? They're as happy as can be," she said.

"They may not have everything they want, but God will bless 'em," Mrs. Tate said. "Everything is going to be all right for Christmas."

Little Shon knew nothing about utility bills. He had just been told that the heater wasn't working. And he certainly couldn't quote St. Francis of Assisi: "For it is in giving that we receive."

He just knew that poor people needed socks. And that he had a pair.

In giving them, a child brought his whole family the warmth of Christmas.

December 24, 1996

Improvement project
is now a labor of love

LIKE A LOT of moms, June Hairston of Duncanville thought her almost-13-year-old daughter needed to focus a little more on others and a little less on herself.

Mrs. Hairston saw a newspaper article about a program in which teens work with mentally retarded youths. So she gave daughter Sherri a firm nudge in that direction.

Needless to say, Sherri wasn't too thrilled with the idea. But she rounded up a few friends to take along and made the best of it.

Last Saturday morning, I joined Sherri at a church in DeSoto as she participated once again in her mama-mandated humanitarian effort.

Not much has changed since her mother first carried Sherri to such a gathering. Except that it truly is voluntary now. And Sherri is able to drive herself to the meetings.

You see, that almost-13-year-old is now almost 42.

And every week for nearly 30 years, she has been hosting activities for mentally retarded friends.

I admire staying power. I can't tell you how many good intentions I've had that never amounted to anything.

And those that did didn't last long.

So my admiration for Sherri is enormous. But she's a down-to-earth sort who just laughed off my praise and blamed it all on her mother. "I think she just decided I was a tad bit self-centered," Sherri said.

She is Sherri Robinson now—a wife and a mother of her own 12-year-old daughter and an 18-year-old son.

That original teen program that Sherri joined soon disbanded. But Sherri couldn't just abandon her new circle of friends. So, with her mom's help, Sherri simply began organizing activities herself.

And she's still at it. Saturday mornings are filled with field trips, bowling, crafts, pizza parties, swimming and Special Olympics practice.

On the morning I visited, it was a popcorn-and-movie day at their home base, DeSoto's Rolling Hills Church of Christ.

As her original group grew older, Sherri didn't want to give the group members up. So she gradually shifted her program from young people to retarded adults.

"There's really more need there anyway," Sherri said. "As long as they are in school, there are lots of activities. But there isn't much in the way of social outings for adults."

One of Sherri's group members, 40-year-old Sherry Dickerson, has been with her from the very beginning. "We went to school together," Sherry told me proudly. At Duncanville's Reed Junior High, it was.

Charlcie Moore has been taking her son, 38-year-old Eric Knott, to Sherri's get-togethers for 20 years now. "There are just not enough good words to say about her," Mrs. Moore said. "She has given so much to our special children."

They are indeed a happy bunch. Last Saturday, a kind of electricity grew in the room as more and more friends arrived—some 40 in all.

Robert was showing off his bowling medal. "I have my own ball!" Megan sat close by her dad, a huge, shy smile across her face. Mike was saying he wants a Cowboys cap for Christmas. Sam, as always, was bad-mouthing the Cowboys. "Just to upset me," Sherri said.

During the week, Sherri cares for infants in her home. But with donations from the community, she somehow also finds time to buy special Christmas gifts for each member of her Saturday group.

For them, Santa's magic never wanes. And as always, Santa will be at next month's Christmas party.

I said that little had changed since Sherri began her good work almost 30 years ago. But one thing has changed.

"Now my mother says, "You're so busy. When are you going to give this up?" Sherri said with a laugh.

In fact, I had intended to ask her why she goes on. But as we talked, Sam, the Cowboy hater, walked by. He stopped and nestled his head on Sherri's shoulder, a gesture of pure affection.

Sherri kept right on talking, but she reached up and gently caressed Sam's face.

And I didn't have to ask why.

November 20, 1998

On the
Soapbox

TALK ABOUT beginner's luck... Even before I began writing the column I knew that I wanted to trumpet the case of Joyce Ann Brown. Her murder conviction was known in cop circles as one of the most troubling. So I began to write about her in my first few weeks on the job. And I discovered that others, too, were quietly working on her behalf. Soon she was released from prison and charges against her dropped.

I wish I could say that I hand in many more such dramatic outcomes. But no, in most cases I mounted the soapbox to no apparent effect.

In truth, I'm not much of a soapbox columnist anyway. The newspaper has never expected me to tell the mayor how to run the city, nor have I ever claimed to know how the mayor ought to run the city. I'm usually so full of conflicted opinions that I couldn't run a stocking.

But here are some cases where I just couldn't resist spouting off. Take them for what they're worth. The job of all journalists, including columnists, is to provide food for your thoughts. Who cares what I say? It's your opinion that matters.

Conviction leaves
doubts that gnaw

THE CRIME was brutal. But mercifully, it looked like an open and shut case.

Two women entered Fine Furs by Rubin on Northwest Highway about 1 p.m. on May 6, 1980. They shot and killed Rubin Danziger, threatened his wife and fled with two trash bags stuffed with furs.

Police recovered the getaway car and found that it had been rented in Denver by Joyce Ann Brown. One cop remembered Joyce Ann Brown. She had a few prostitution convictions in Dallas. And they learned that she was working at another Dallas furrier, Koslow's.

Ala Danziger identified photos of Ms. Brown and Rene Taylor as the two women who left her husband dead.

Ms. Brown was found guilty of aggravated robbery and sentenced to life in prison, where she has remained for eight years.

"I've never seen so many coincidences to lead police to what seemed a cut-and-dried case," said Kerry FitzGerald, the court-appointed lawyer who represented Ms. Brown.

But in FitzGerald's mind and in many others', the case is far from cut and dried.

"I'm just totally convinced that she is innocent," he said.

It's hard to believe that yet another innocent person could have been sent to prison from Dallas County. We all know about the Lenell Geter case. And now Randall Dale Adams may soon go free.

Surely there can't be another.

Yet Joyce Ann Brown comes up whenever cops or lawyers or reporters begin talking about troubling cases.

For FitzGerald, the case is a knot in his gut that won't go away. "In the realm of cases that bother me, it's at the top of the list," he said.

He also thought it was an open and shut case at first. "But then I saw the evidence start to crumble," he said.

For starters, police learned that the car had been rented by another Joyce Ann Brown. That woman, a Denver resident, said she had lent the car to her friend Rene Taylor.

Ms. Taylor later pleaded guilty to the robbery and was sentenced to life in prison.

When police searched the getaway car, they found Ms. Taylor's fingerprints but none belonging to Ms. Brown. No physical evidence was found linking Ms. Brown to the crime.

And four Koslow's employees came forward to testify that Ms. Brown was at work around the time of the 1 p.m. robbery. One remembered seeing her about 12:40 p.m. Another spoke with her at 1:20 p.m.

And they testified that she wore a white skirt and black blouse to work that day. The bandit wore a blue jogging suit.

But prosecutors contended that Ms. Brown had time to travel the three miles to the Danzigers' store, commit the crime and return to work, changing clothes somewhere along the way.

And prosecutors had the dramatic, tearful testimony of Ala Danziger. She said it was Ms. Brown who watched as the other bandit shot her husband as he begged for his life.

"My heart goes out to her," FitzGerald said. "She is obviously trying to act in good faith, but she's obviously wrong."

FitzGerald has no such charity toward a final surprise witness in the trial. Martha Jean Bruce, who was in jail at the time on unrelated charges, testified that Ms. Brown told her in jail that she committed the crime.

Ms. Bruce said prosecutors promised her nothing in exchange for her testimony. But two months later, then-District Attorney Henry Wade asked the state parole board to reduce Ms. Bruce's five-year sentence to two.

The request was granted, and she went free seven months later. FitzGerald continues plugging away at the case. Ms. Brown has passed two lie-detector tests. Rene Taylor passed another, saying Ms. Brown wasn't involved.

For FitzGerald, the case has become an affront to our legal system.

State District Judge Ron Chapman, who tried the case, said it still sticks in his mind. "I am somewhat troubled that people who I respect are sincere in their belief that this lady is not guilty," he said.

But not everyone is troubled. Does prosecutor Norman Kinne have any doubts?

"No," he said curtly.

And would he elaborate?

"No," he said.

February 22, 1989

King's dream transcends
racial lines

AFTER MY grandmother died in the spring of 1966, we began renting out her small frame house. It fell to my father to serve as landlord over this humble piece of real estate.

His primary chore—and therefore mine as well—was to periodically clean up the squalor left behind by another batch of sorry renters. Inevitably, they would leave the house in shambles and owing a few months rent.

One Saturday as we worked outside the house, a middle-aged black man came walking up the driveway. As I recall, he held a brimmed hat in his hands.

He had parked his car at the curb. His wife and several small children watched from the car, their faces pressed against the windows.

Dad greeted him, and the man seemed to momentarily summon his courage before asking if the house was available for rent.

It was a question that took some courage. In the mid-1960s in East Texas, the civil rights movement was just something happening on our television screens. It had not yet arrived with any force.

A small creek ran just a stone's throw from my grandmother's house. That was the boundary line for "colored town."

This man hoped to move his family to the better homes just across that creek. He hoped to break a taboo as old as the South. The effort was painful to behold.

I watched as he apologized and fumbled with his question. And I watched as my father apologized and fumbled with his answer.

My father said no. He could not rent the house to the man.

My adolescent anger rose as I heard him lamely explain that he certainly had no objections personally, but that most of the neighbors were elderly and he feared they would oppose it. In fact, the widow next door had specifically asked my father not to rent to a black family.

The man was perfectly polite. He said he understood, thanked Dad for his time and walked back down the driveway to his waiting family.

I don't remember what I said to Dad as we returned to our chores. But I was mad at him for not renting the house, for not practicing the equality he had always preached. Yet I understood his predicament. And I was mad at myself for understanding.

I could see that Dad was also mad at himself for having been put in that position. And angry about losing what undoubtedly would have been a better renter than the previous string of ne'er-do-wells.

That incident was an important one for me—crystallizing in a few anguished moments what the civil rights movement was all about.

But I hadn't thought of the incident in years. Not until a few days ago.

My wife and I have been house hunting for a few months. The other day, a real estate agent showed us a lovely home on the outskirts of the city.

As we stood outside the house, admiring the wide-open spaces, the real estate agent turned to us and said, "Yep, if you buy this house, you can be sure you won't have any negroids or chinks moving in next to you."

A slap in the face could not have stung me more.

Was that really what he thought we sought in a house? Or worse, was that simply part of his standard sales pitch?

It left me disheartened for days, wondering whether we will ever live in racial harmony.

Tomorrow, of course, is Martin Luther King Day. It is a day for those people who are oppressed by prejudice.

And now I realize, that is all of us.

I went back and read Dr. King's famous "I Have A Dream" speech. When he spoke of being "free at last, free at last," he did not simply mean people of color. He meant "all of God's children, black men and white men, Jews and Gentiles, Protestants and Catholics."

He meant freedom for that man who wanted to rent my grandmother's home. And he meant freedom for my father to rent it to him.

He meant freedom for the real estate agent who thought he needed racism to help close a sale—but lost a sale instead.

He meant freedom for the black leaders who now stand at City Hall and cry out against racism. And he meant freedom from the whites whose hearts are hardened by those cries.

He dreamed of freedom for us all.

January 14, 1990

In the game of Poverty,
no one wins

WE ALL KNOW what it's like to be rich. After all, everyone has played Monopoly.

But maybe it would be helpful if more of us also knew what it's like to be poor. Well, perhaps there is a way we can.

After consulting with social workers to assure complete authenticity, I'm ready to unveil a new product. Grab those dice and get ready to play the fun new game: "Poverty"

START HERE: You have worked 10 years in the same manufacturing plant. Today the boss announced that the plant will move to Malaysia. The good news is that you get two weeks' severance pay. Roll the dice, and good luck.

Your spouse has been out of work six months. Now you're both looking for a job. That's too bad. Lose your turn.

What? No high school diploma? Most employers want at least a GED. Go back one space.

The severance pay is gone. Welcome to the world of welfare. You've got your AFDC and your WIC and your SSI and your food stamps. Or maybe you don't qualify at all. Spend three days filling out forms.

After waiting two weeks, you meet with food-stamps caseworker. Oops—no birth certificate for your oldest child? Sorry, come back when you find it.

You land job as part-time clerk in convenience store. No medical insurance. No benefits. You bring home $100 a week. Move ahead one space.

Now that you're working, welfare benefits are reduced by $90 a week. Go back two spaces.

Your spouse answers an ad for "entry-level marketing job." It's telephone sales of storm windows. $140 a week take-home. Move ahead one space.

Congratulations. You're both working. Now fork over $90 a week for child care. Go back one space.

Your daughter wakes up with high fever. Go to the free clinic at the county hospital. Phone boss to say you'll be a little late.

Five hours later, you're still waiting at the free clinic. The waiting room is stuffy and crowded. Phone boss to say you won't make it in today. He says don't bother coming back. Go back to START.

Car breaks down. No money for repairs. Spouse spends two hours riding bus and walking to crosstown job. You look for work by bus. Very inefficient. Lose turn.

Utility bills are piling up. To save money, give up telephone. Very frugal. Move ahead one space.

No telephone? Sorry, but without a phone number to put on job applications, your chances of landing a job are nearly zero. Tough luck. Go back three spaces.

Eviction Notice: You have 24 hours to vacate these premises for non-payment of rent. Contact public housing authority. Join six-month waiting list.

Your spouse arrives for work at phone marketing firm. It is closed and padlocked. No forwarding address. No chance of getting two weeks' back pay.

Pride won't let you take family to downtown shelter. Begin sleeping in disabled car.

People stare at family living in car. One man says so you can hear, "God helps those who help themselves."

Hopelessness and despair set in. You lose. Poverty wins. Remain on this spot forever.

November 4, 1990

U.S. is still
the train to bountiful

ABOUT FIVE years ago, as a reporter for this newspaper, I was assigned to help cover the pope's visit to San Antonio. I was thrilled with my particular assignment.

A special overnight passenger train was created to carry people to San Antonio for the Sunday Mass, and I was to ride along.

The train—made up of old, restored passenger cars—was dubbed the Papal Eagle, and I thought nothing could be more romantic.

We pulled out shortly before midnight, and the train rocked along through the night, picking up more pilgrims in towns along the way.

I roamed the train, talking to people positively giddy with excitement over this adventure.

As the night wore on, however, the romance of the rails began to give way to the realities. The train was running well behind schedule. The plumbing balked. The air conditioning fizzled. The cars became rolling saunas.

And so, after a night of very little sleep, we arrived in San Antonio on Sunday morning for the outdoor Mass. It was a day of blistering heat, long hikes and massive crowds.

By the time everyone got back to the train Sunday evening, we were one bedraggled group.

As the train started out on the long trip home, the mood was decidedly glum. Lots of people wished to abandon the romance of the rails for the speed of Southwest Airlines.

The mood on that train reminds me of the mood in this city and in this country right now. People feel disappointed and dispirited.

Of course, the most pressing heartache is the Rodney King verdict and its aftermath. But the discontent goes much deeper.

Political candidates all begin to sound alike. Washington seems gridlocked by competing self-interests. After years of struggle, racial relations seem only worse. Here at home, we lurch from one controversy to the next.

In short, it feels like we're all stuck on a hot, creaking train to nowhere.

That's sure how it felt that Sunday evening in San Antonio. As the sun was setting, I stepped out onto the platform between cars for a breath of fresh air.

I stood there, feeling sorry for myself, watching the streets and neighborhoods of San Antonio slip by. And then I began to notice something—all the faces looking back at me were smiling.

In the cars stopped at the railroad crossings, the faces behind the windshields beamed at seeing the special train go by. Children in back yards ran and waved and called out at the sight of this odd, mismatched train.

Suddenly, as if lifted by a cool breeze, my spirit soared. I wasn't trapped on that train, I was lucky to be on that train.

Even with all the little hardships involved, those smiling faces reminded me that it was a privilege to be aboard the Papal Eagle. And for the rest of the trip, I relished the chance to sit back and relax, read, nap and chat with new friends.

America is a lot like that train. Sometimes we feel overwhelmed by our problems. We feel trapped. And worse, we let ourselves begin to feel powerless.

But we forget that most of the world watches the United States with smiling faces, with a mixture of awe and envy. We're not trapped in this nation, we're lucky to be here.

Imagine: One of our major problems is that so many other people want to come here. They want desperately to get on board this train.

Yes, sometimes our criminal justice system seems to let more crooks go free than it keeps—including some bad cops. But we also enjoy the greatest protections on Earth from unwarranted prosecution.

No, our governmental institutions never quite live up to our expectations. But for the most part, they are failings of human frailty, not the corruption and thievery that cripple so many other governments.

And true, our racial struggles never quite seem to solve the problem. But even in the midst of riot, the mass of people still work peacefully to find unity and equity.

It's not a perfect train we share. Far from it. But it's among the best yet devised. And we're still in charge to direct its course.

May 3, 1992

Looking beyond
gay stereotypes

AWHILE BACK I wrote a column that touched on AIDS and homosexuality. And, as usual, the mail brought a pile of anti-gay letters.

As I sat at home one evening, answering them, I suddenly wondered why my feelings on the subject should be so different from those of the letter writers.

What would explain why some people feel such hostility toward gays while I feel none?

As I pondered the question, an unexpected answer struck me.

Let's use the names Robert and Harold.

I hadn't thought of them in a long time. And I hadn't seen them since childhood. But I knew they had to be the answer.

Long before I knew there was such a thing as homosexuality, I knew Robert and Harold. They went to my church.

I grew up in a very small, old-fashioned, old-time-religion kind of church. I'm sure that if someone had asked whether homosexuality is a sin, the answer would have been yes.

But more powerful than what was preached in our little church was what was practiced. And that was complete acceptance of Robert and Harold.

How could we not? They were part of our church family.

Robert grew up in the Tyler church, just as my mother had. Everyone had known him since he was a boy. His mother was one of the pillars of the church, the perennial leader of the Women's Missionary Society.

And then one day he began bringing Harold to church. Harold had a beautiful voice and often sang solos—"specials" we called them. Normally we had only congregational singing in our church.

One year, Harold directed the church Christmas program. I was so proud because he gave me one of the "big roles.' I wore a Christmas sweater and sat casually—sort of Perry Como-style—on the altar steps and read a holiday poem from one of those Ideals books.

Now that's entertainment!

I don't remember how I learned that Robert and Harold were gay. It seems like Mom or Dad just casually mentioned it one day.

I couldn't summon too much shock. After all, I had known them all my life. They had always seemed like nice, normal people before. And they continued to seem like nice, normal people.

Thinking about it today, I have to admit that if I had never known Robert and Harold, I might feel the same way as those angry letter writers. If all my images of gays came from TV—drag queens and angry militants and foppish hair-dressers—then I, too, might regard homosexuality as something frightening and perverse.

But I know that not all heterosexuals are represented by Madonna or Jimmy Swaggart or, heaven forbid, TV's Studs. And I know that the stereotypes don't represent gays and lesbians.

And I will confess that if I let my thoughts dwell too long on bedroom activities, I can feel a certain shudder of revulsion at homosexuality. I suppose that becomes the basis of some people's hatred.

But what that shudder tells me is that sexual orientation goes to the very core of our being. It is deep-seated and complex and certainly not just a "bad choice," as Vice President Dan Quayle was saying during the political campaign.

(Or at least it's not a choice for me. I don't know about Mr. Quayle. Maybe he watches, say, "Pretty Woman" and chooses whether to be attracted to Julia Roberts or Richard Gere. But I doubt it.)

I realize that most people don't get the chance to know a Robert and Harold. Or at least they don't know that they do.

That's the irony, of course. A lot of people rant against "those perverts." Meanwhile, they are surrounded every day by quiet, decent, hard-working people who also happen to be gay.

Earlier this year, I was saddened to hear the news that Harold had passed away.

No, it wasn't AIDS. It was just the usual assortment of health problems that go with growing older.

Robert and Harold had shared a life together for 36 years.

I don't pretend to have answers to all the mysteries and moral complexities of homosexuality. And I don't offer these thoughts to advance "a homosexual agenda,' as some will argue.

But I know that where some people see monsters, I see Robert and Harold—a couple of nice, normal people.

November 29, 1992

OK, parents, time
to make, follow rules

A TEACHERS' group foolishly asked me to make a few remarks the other evening. And as I was pondering what I might say, the phrase "crisis in education" kept coming to mind.

It's a given these days that our schools are in a mess.

But as I thought about it, it suddenly dawned on me that we don't really have a "crisis in education."

What we have is a "crisis in parenting."

And that's what I told the group that night—that we're focusing on the wrong crisis. And the amazing thing is, the more I think about it, the more I think I was actually right.

If we as parents were able to send happy, healthy, well-disciplined, well-supervised children to school, there would be no "crisis in education."

Teachers would be teaching instead of spending all their time trying to fix our failures as parents.

I'm not saying schools are perfect. But maybe it's time we quit dumping everything on education and got real honest with each other about the job we're doing as parents.

Maybe we ought to be holding each other to a little higher standard of responsible parenthood.

To that end, I'll start by offering a few things I'd like to see parents doing—some big, some small. And mind you, I'm not holding myself out as an expert. I've got two kids ready to prove otherwise at any moment.

But I am willing to crawl up on the soapbox first to exhort us on. You be thinking about the things you want to say.

* No R-rated Movies: It's pitiful, but Hollywood is more morally responsible than we are. They put R ratings on movies to plainly say they're not fit for kids, and then we go and take our kids to the movies or let them rent the videos or watch on cable. Let's agree: No R-rated movies for kids. They rot young minds.

* Midnight Curfew: The City Council shouldn't have to tell us when our kids need to be home. We should be doing it. There's an old

saying: "Nothing good happens after midnight." If we stick together, we can make this work—teen-agers home by midnight.

* Go to Church: Yeah, I know, it can be boring and a lot of hypocrites are there and it's hard to get up on Sunday morning and it's tough to find a good church. Do it anyway. Your kids need it. You need it. You might even like it.

* Turn Off the TV: Get up from your chair. Go outside with your child. Find something to do. Throw a ball. Pull weeds. Make paper airplanes. Race to the corner. Talk.

* Discipline Well: Don't yell. Don't scream. Don't slap. Don't punch. Set rules. Set punishments. Stick to them. Stay calm. It's not easy. It's hard. If you need help, call the Warm-line for Parents (972-699-7742).

* Get Married: It takes two people to become parents. It takes two people to be parents. If you're not married, don't have babies. Get a puppy.

* Stay Married: Remember that quaint old phrase—"staying married for the kids." There was some genius in that. It saved a lot of kids. And a lot of good marriages.

* Say "No" Sometimes: It's always easier to say "yes." It hurts to say "no." But kids need to hear it. Practice these phrases—"Because you don't need it," "Because it's too expensive," "Because we can't afford it."

* Say "Yes" Sometimes.

* Teach Respect: People in authority may not always be right, but they deserve respect. It's true for teachers. It's true for police officers. It's true for presidents. Teach your children by example to disagree agreeably. Teach your children that life won't always seem fair.

* Love Abundantly: Hug. Kiss. Compliment. Praise. Pat. They may pretend they don't like it. Don't fall for it.

* Have Fun: Lighten up. Laugh off the mishaps. Save some of those chores for tomorrow. Sit in the floor and play a game. It's all over so soon.

OK, there's my sermon. Now it's your turn. Tell me where parents are failing. Be practical. Be philosophical.

But most of all, be blunt. The schools can't cover for us much longer.

April 10, 1994

Parental nerve hit
by crisis column

BOY, DID I hit a nerve!

In last Sunday's column, I said I had come to the conclusion that the much-discussed "crisis in education" isn't our real problem. What we have is a "crisis in parenting."

It looks like I was the last one to figure that out.

Hundreds of you wrote and called last week. Many simply wanted to say amen and hooray. Many more sent suggestions for fixing this mess. It's no surprise that teachers especially liked the column.

A few quibbled with my own list of recommendations. They were important, so let's get to them first.

I said people need to get married and stay married—that there was value in that old idea of "staying married for the kids." But several wrote to say from experience that good parents sometimes must find the courage to end a destructive marriage.

And some single parents said they felt dumped on once again. "I hear the unanimous voice of people like you bewailing the 'single-parent home' as if this is a fate worse than death. It does not have to be. It depends on the integrity of the single parent in providing a stable living environment for his/her children," wrote Lanelle Latendresse of Dallas.

She's right, of course. A lot of great kids are raised by single parents.

Now let's get to some of your suggestions, big and small. I wish I had room to print them all.

* Teach Responsibility: This was probably the top suggestion. But how to do it? Give kids regular household chores. Don't let them blame others for their problems. And let them suffer the consequences of their irresponsibility. Don't run that forgotten book/lunch money/homework back to school. Don't do that science project for them at midnight. Don't appeal to the teacher for a second chance. To teach success, let them fail. (Oooh, that's hard.)

* Take Charge: You are the parent. So act like it. "To be blunt, parents today need to lay down strict, distinct boundaries for their children and STICK TO THEM!," wrote 22-year-old Amy Rader of DeSoto, an adult young enough to remember what kids really want. "Let

your child know that you are in charge. I see so many parents today that appear to be afraid of their children."

* Read to Your Children: And when they get older, keep reading.

* Apologize: When you goof with your children (and you will), admit it and apologize. "It's very difficult for a child to stay angry with a humble parent," Janey Hall of Richardson wrote.

* Eat Together: Somehow, some way, get your whole family together at dinner time. Turn off the TV. Sit down. Relax. Eat. Talk. Smile. Listen. (I suspect this may be more powerful than any of us realizes.)

* Put Your Children First: No business meeting is more important. No golf game, fishing trip, happy hour or weekend getaway. "We have become selfish, non-sacrificing overachievers, and parenting is a part-time business proposition instead of a moral obligation to our children," wrote Jeanne Frank of Irving.

* Drugs and Alcohol: "Kids learn by example. Set a good one," writes a recovering alcoholic who is the child of an alcoholic. "If you drink excessively, use drugs, eat too much, smoke, etc., don't be surprised if your children follow in your footsteps."

* Be a Team: If you have disagreements about parenting (and you will), iron them out in private. Never in front of the kids. Support each other. And for heaven's sake, divorced parents, quit fighting through your kids. Sure, you hate each other. Do you want your kids to hate you, too?

* Go Easy: "Remember that children are not 'short adults,' " wrote Judy Stout of Forney.

* Be Consistent: Don't blow off steam with idle threats. If you say it, mean it. "Follow through every time on what you say you will or will not do . . . ," wrote Clara Ann Norman of Richardson.

* Teach Manners: "Please." "Thank you." Remember those?

* Be An Example: Here's the very toughest. In your every word and deed, children are learning to be just like you. Scary, isn't it?

God bless us all.

April 17, 1994

Intolerance is never
the right answer

AWHILE BACK, I was asked an intriguing question. And I've been rethinking my answer ever since.

I had spoken to a youth group about careers in journalism and then answered a few questions from the kids—the usual ones, "Where do you get your ideas?" "Have you ever met Troy Aikman?"

I was about to sit down—and the kids were ready for me to—when one of the mothers in the group raised her hand for a final question:

"What do you think is the greatest threat facing these young people in the future?"

Wow, what a fascinating, profound, challenging question! (I was in big trouble.)

My mind raced through some possibilities. Well, let's see, "nuclear war" is always a good answer. But I guess that was really my generation's greatest threat.

I thought about saying "the environment." Nothing else matters if we go into global meltdown. And it's a nice, safe answer. But I couldn't honestly call that the greatest threat.

Finally, I blurted out this improbable reply: "Intolerance."

I'm still not exactly sure where that came from. But I told that mother and the kids that the only thing separating this society from the Middle East or Northern Ireland or Bosnia is our willingness to tolerate differences in each other.

The only thing that stands between peace and war is our willingness to settle our differences with words instead of weapons.

And I told them that I see dwindling tolerance and a frightening increase in hostility between people of opposing views.

I'm sure those kids remember me only as that reporter who never met Troy Aikman. But I've been pondering my answer ever since. And here's the weird part: I think I stand by it.

This all comes to mind again because of the latest killings at the abortion clinics—the latest example of someone who exchanged words for a weapon.

The plain truth is that there's not much premium placed on tolerance these days.

Remember that noble quote we all learned in school: "I disapprove of what you say, but I will defend to the death your right to say it."

I'm afraid the modern American version is: "I disapprove of what you say, so SHUT UP!!!"

I realize that some might say the biggest threat to our young people is too much tolerance—too much tolerance of violence and immorality, too much tolerance of poverty and inequity.

And there's some truth to that.

But I still believe the greater threat, the thing that could cripple this society, is the seductive path of intolerance.

It says that people who disagree with us aren't just wrong, they are evil. They aren't just opponents, they are the enemy.

And don't try to read any ideological slant here. I'm seeing this mindset across the political and social spectrum. That's what makes it dangerous: It's contagious.

We long for "traditional values." And it does seem that tolerance is one of the forgotten parts of our national character.

It's been a long time since I heard anyone shrug off an unpopular view with, "It takes all kinds to make the world go 'round."

It's been a long time since I heard someone refuse to criticize with the adage, "Live and let live."

I realize that our tolerance is now tested to new limits in this crazy-quilt society. When I was growing up in East Texas, our idea of diversity was Baptist and Methodist.

And please understand that when I talk about tolerance, that's not the same thing as approval—or even acceptance. And it doesn't mean you have to sit by in silence. By all means, speak up. State your case. Join the debate.

That's what democracy is all about. But it's also about shaking hands and walking away with confidence that wisdom and right will prevail.

You often hear people talk about something being "the glue that holds us together." They might be talking about patriotism or integrity or whatever.

But the truth is that we're really not glued together in one big lump. We're a nation of 260 million people and just that many different opinions.

And tolerance is the grease that lets us get along.

January 8, 1995

They lived happily ever after? Pffft

IT SUDDENLY occurred to me the other day that we have been poisoning children's minds for generations.

We do it with this: *And they lived happily ever after . . .*

What an insidious little phrase that is.

I know I'm not the first person to muse on this. You hear adults use that phrase in a sarcastic way all the time.

But I'm not sure we fully realize the impact those lyrical words have on us in our tender years. By the time we know enough to be sarcastic, the damage is already done.

As children, we truly take that notion to heart, living happily ever after. I mean, who could resist such a beautiful idea?

Then, as adults, whether we want to admit it or not, some part of us clings to that magical hope. Every time things go wrong, we manage to be surprised all over again.

Can you tell we've had a lot of surprises at our house lately?

When the washer overflowed, I was surprised. When the lawn mower started gushing gasoline, I was surprised. When the weed trimmer ran out of line, I was mildly surprised. When I couldn't find the spool of replacement line I had just bought, I was very surprised.

When the air conditioning suddenly sputtered, I was surprised. When my daughter called the other night and said her car was stalled in the middle of an intersection, I was surprised.

Boy, was I surprised when I got into my car the other day and the air conditioner wouldn't work and the power windows wouldn't go down.

That was a very warm surprise.

My wife had 50 fellow teachers at our house for lunch Friday. Shortly beforehand, she discovered that the oven wasn't working. (Hey, even stuff from Sam's has to be heated.)

She's resourceful. She had peach cobblers baking in friends' ovens all over eastern Dallas County. And she was very, very surprised.

Yet somehow, after every mishap, we wonder again: Now do we start living happily ever after?

When I was talking to Zig Ziglar for a column the other day, he said something that struck me as truly profound.

Mr. Ziglar is famous, of course, for his positive outlook, for his see-you-at-the-top system of successful thinking. But he believes a little clear-eyed, hard-nosed realism is also vital. And here's what he said: "Unrealistic expectations are the seedbed of depression."

And they lived happily ever after. . . . Man, that's a whole hayfield of depression.

We stubbornly hang on to the idea that once we achieve or acquire a certain thing, that will make us live happily ever after. You fill in the blank—a husband, a wife, a new one, rich, richer, thin, thinner, taller, shorter, a house, a bigger house, a smaller house, children, grown children.

And if there's anything worse than clinging to the idea of living happily ever after, it's deciding that only other people manage to achieve pure happiness.

There's a comment I hear periodically that really troubles me. Readers will say something to the effect, "You have such a perfect little family."

I'm sure they mean well, but I feel like such a fraud. And a bad journalist. I'm supposed to be dealing in truth here. Obviously, I have failed spectacularly.

Listen, just because I don't sort and stack dirty laundry in this space doesn't mean we don't have hamper loads at home.

My only consolation is the assurance that most of you do, too.

Now, don't get me wrong. I haven't renounced my Pollyanna membership. I won't be buying one of those T-shirts: "Life's a bitch and then you die."

But I do love a story that Rose-Mary Rumbley tells in her book, *An Unauthorized History of Dallas.*

The book really isn't history so much as a charming remembrance of Rose-Mary's mother, Amy Hass Brau.

Mrs. Brau was one of the pillars of the First Baptist Church. She was a woman of class and refinement, certainly not one given to coarse language.

But Rose-Mary says that one of the most valuable lessons she ever learned in life came when something had gone wrong. Her mother heaved a big sigh and said to her, "Honey, life is one damn thing after another."

The trick is living happily in between.

July 30, 1995

Hollywood, take a lesson
from the men's room

MY WIFE AND I went to the movies the other night with our son and his girlfriend.

Our first double date!

It was a lot of fun (though I'm now picturing Corey roll his eyes at the nerd words "double date").

As we watched the movie, there came one of those front-porch scenes. You know, the kiss at the end of a first date and the old "should he come in" debate.

Of course it's a given in the movies these days that any discussion of "coming in" is in fact a decision of whether there will be sex.

And so, as the two characters kissed at the doorstep and debated whether he should come in, I found myself sitting there silently screaming at the screen:

"No! Don't do it! Please! Don't go in! It's your first date. My son and his girlfriend are sitting right here. Be good role models! Just say, 'Good night.' Ple-e-ease?"

He went in.

Of course he went in. How could I have possibly hoped otherwise? There were no sex scenes or anything. Just the usual coy waking-up-the-next-morning scene.

Suddenly I remembered something that I had seen a few days earlier. It was a message that I had read on, of all things, a condom machine.

OK, I know this is weird. But I was in a restroom and there was this condom machine on the wall right in front of my nose, if you know what I mean.

So as I stood there, I could hardly avoid reading the standard line about condoms being protection against the spread of AIDS and other sexually transmitted diseases.

But then, incredibly, it went on to say: "The best method of AIDS prevention is abstinence before marriage and a monogamous relationship during marriage."

How quaint!

And isn't it strange that one would find better guidance on sexual relations on a condom machine than in a mainstream American movie?

This all came to mind again the other night as my family watched "Friends." In the episode, Phoebe ran upstairs to complain to the new guy in the apartment above that he was too noisy.

The next night they listened as Phoebe had noisy sex with the new guy in the apartment above. (Ha. Ha. Big laugh track.)

Then the real knee-slapper came the next night when Phoebe and friends heard the new guy upstairs having sex with someone else! Oh, what hilarity. What madcap comedy.

And I couldn't help thinking about the message imparted to my two teenagers.

I'd like to suggest some future episodes of "Friends." How about "Phoebe, Meet Chlamydia." That would be a stitch, wouldn't it?

Or maybe "Phoebe Makes Up Her Mind: Adoption, Abortion, a Parent?" The new guy upstairs could give comic reactions to facing 20 percent deductions from his paycheck for child support.

What fun. Or why not really be relevant: "Phoebe Dies of AIDS." At least 14,000 women in this country got AIDS last year.

There is another reality out there that Hollywood isn't dealing with, and it's this: Casual sex isn't cool anymore.

"Free love" was my generation's bad idea. The next generation is wiser. A new survey of college freshmen finds that approval of casual sex has dwindled ever lower.

Sex-ed programs are actually talking about abstinence now. And teens welcome it! They are pleased to hear someone say it's OK to stand apart from this hyper-sexualized society of ours.

I've teased about us Southern Baptists and our tendency to look like the crabbiest people on Earth. But one of the things I'm most proud of as a Baptist is a little program on sexuality for teens. My two kids and thousands of others of many faiths have now heard the message.

And it's all summed up in three little words: "True Love Waits."

Aren't those beautiful words?

It's not about shaking a finger at kids. It's not about sermonizing or moralizing. It's not a bunch of "Thou Shalt Nots . . . ."

It's about admitting that my generation made a lot of mistakes. And that there is a path to happier, healthier, deeper sexual fulfillment.

True love waits. Maybe someday in the movies, too.

January 19, 1997

Sometimes, being
wrong isn't so bad

I TACKLED the weeds in the front flower bed one morning last week. As I worked, I thought about the hoe in my hands.

I think I actually laughed out loud when Dad passed it along to me a year or so ago.

At the time, we were busy cleaning out storage rooms and dividing stuff among the kids as Mom and Dad prepared to move to a townhome.

The garden hoe was among some things Dad had gotten in a similar division of goods at a great-uncle's house years before.

I couldn't help but laugh a little at the funny ways of old folks. I couldn't believe that Dad had bothered keeping the hoe. Or that my uncle had, for that matter.

You see, over the years, the hoe had been filed and filed until the blade was now just a tiny sliver of steel.

(Only older folks raised in the cotton patch persist in filing hoes, a labor-saving step forgotten by my generation.)

"Trash," I thought to myself as I gathered up that worn-out hoe. "And aren't old folks funny?"

Well, you can probably guess the rest. I have a couple of nice, newer hoes hanging in the garage. But about the only one I use these days is that silly nub of a hoe.

As I scratched around the verbena in that front flower bed, I marveled again at what a perfect, agile size it is. And how wrong I had been.

It occurs to me as I settle into undeniable middle age that one of the real pleasures of life these days is discovering when I'm wrong.

Once I was always right. And how tedious that was.

Maybe it's that whole Father Knows Best philosophy we all grew up with. Or maybe, as my loving wife says, I'm just opinionated and obnoxious. But for a long time I labored under the idea that it really was my duty to know best.

Whether it was choosing a movie, a restaurant or the course of humanity, I felt a responsibility to know the wiser choice.

Oh, I still think I know. But now, when someone disagrees, I usually go with the flow. And life is infinitely more fun.

It's amazing how often I'm delighted to discover I was wrong.

On a family vacation to Washington, D.C., a few years ago, I had done the dad thing and worked out an hour-by-hour sightseeing itinerary.

My teenage son had been sort of ho-hum about the whole trip, but Corey suddenly decided he wanted to see the Senate and the House of Representatives.

Well, I was dead set against it. It wasn't on my itinerary. It's a big hassle. You have to find the office of your representative or senators, get a pass, stand in line . . . .

It turned out to be the highlight of the trip. The whole experience was terrific fun. Visiting the offices. Riding the little underground trolley. Watching as some poor guy delivered a speech to the empty House. Listening as senators debated foreign policy toward China.

I don't even remember what we missed on my itinerary. But it was great being wrong.

Mom was saying the other day that she and Dad once read about the three little magic words that are the secret to a happy marriage. And they really worked, she said.

"I love you?"

Nope, something more powerful: "Maybe you're right."

It's not exactly like admitting you're wrong. It's just a way of remembering we're seldom completely right.

Wouldn't the tenor of our public debate be much nicer with the tempering effect of those three little words?

There's one area where I was troubled by this growing awareness of my wrongness—in matters of religion.

My mounting uncertainties caused real consternation, especially as I looked around and saw others who seemed so hellfire certain about every detail of God's desires.

Was my faith too shallow?

No, I finally decided. My faith is deep enough to confront my ignorance before the awesome mysteries of God. And maybe that humility honors God best.

It's a lot to think about while hoeing weeds out of the flower bed. But those are my views these days.

I might be completely wrong.

May 31, 1998

Adventures
Fast and Slow

OK, I'LL CONFESS. I didn't go into journalism to protect truth, justice and the American way of life. I just liked the press pass.

Oh, there may have been some of that do-gooder stuff mixed in there, too. But mostly I realized early on that journalism is a ticket to do all sorts of fun stuff on the job. That's the sort of high-minded journalism you will find here.

Actually the dear-old press pass doesn't really exist any more. As ethical standards in the business have improved, the freebies have mostly disappeared. But even with the newspaper picking up the tab, the job has allowed me to go off on all sorts of adventures, from jet speed to foot speed. I hope readers have enjoyed coming along for the ride.

This research was definitely hard-hitting

WHEN YOUNG people ask me about the secret to good journalism (pretending for a moment that they do), I answer, "Research! Tireless research!"

Which explains why I was standing in a wicker basket one evening this week as it grew buoyant beneath my feet.

Oh sure, I could have written about this weekend's Mesquite Balloon Festival from a press release and a few phone calls. It's the biggest such event in the state, with some 80 hot-air balloons scheduled to participate.

But to truly grasp the essence of the subject, I was willing to spend an evening flying in a hot-air balloon. And what a happy coincidence! It's something I've always wanted to do. (But was too cheap to pay for.)

So there I stood Wednesday evening, shoulder to shoulder with balloon pilot and festival organizer Jack Nelson, in a basket beneath a billowing balloon in a vacant field behind a Wendy's and a Texaco station in Mesquite.

This takeoff spot had been carefully chosen because the wind direction indicated that we would drift to the southwest and land in Mesquite's Paschall Park. Maybe.

"There's a chance we could hit the park from here," Dr. Nelson said. "Or we may hit the Trail Dust Steakhouse. That would be OK. It's all-you-can-eat night."

When the balloon was rigged and ready, Dr. Nelson said, "Hop on in."

I scrambled aboard as he fired periodic blasts from the propane burner. Each time, an enormous tongue of fire belched up into the translucent bulb of fabric rising seven stories above us.

Gradually, the basket began to tip and sway, dancing at equilibrium with gravity.

"We're getting close to flying temperature," he said. A gauge indicated that the temperature at the top of the balloon was approaching 200 degrees.

Suddenly, we were aloft. Not flying, just floating. Drifting off like a cloud.

Dr. Nelson waved broadly to the receding crowd of people. His other hand, in a leather work glove, rested on the burner controls. He looked like the engineer on some mystical flying locomotive.

The propane burner belched frequently, and we sailed above a residential area. Children's voices rose up in excitement at our approach.

The sound of barking dogs came from every direction. The canine alarm was being sounded: A fire-breathing behemoth was invading the neighborhood.

On and on we drifted.

Dr. Nelson has been flying balloons for 12 years. "It's a good way to relax," he said.

"And it's challenging every time you go. For instance, am I going to land here—or over there?' he said, pointing first to a field just short of LBJ Freeway, then to another across the freeway.

We began descending sharply. "Are you going to land here?" I asked. "I think so," he said.

We skirted a gulley and touched down near a line of trees—rapidly approaching trees. The basket hopped along the ground. "We're going back up," he said, and the propane burner roared. We gained altitude, but not quite quickly enough. The basket crashed through the tree tops. On up we went, over the freeway. Cars honked.

"We'll land there," he said, pointing to a stingy scrap of ground, the only empty patch in sight. He had said he could land on a baseball diamond. I hadn't envisioned that power lines would stretch from first to second to third.

Now we were descending really fast. Dr. Nelson yanked at a yellow line that opened the top of the balloon and allowed hot air to spill out.

"Hang on," he said. "We're going to bounce." Much like an anvil bounces.

We crashed hard to the ground, and the basket toppled over. I felt my left ankle fold a degree or two too far. "That was a pinpoint landing," Dr. Nelson said as we lay there on the ground.

Later he would concede that he had come down harder than usual in that less-than-ideal landing field. "When I ripped the top out, it really nailed us to the ground," he said.

The research had proved even more hard-hitting than I had imagined, but I thanked him nonetheless.

The balloon festival runs through Sunday. I'll be limping through Monday.

July 7, 1989

Hold the G's
on the next flight, please

I ANSWERED the phone several weeks ago, and a woman said, "I hear you're going to fly the highway to the danger zone."

Reacting quickly, I said, "Huh?"

"I hear you've been nominated to fly with the Blue Angels," she said.

Oh, right. My editor had mentioned the idea. The Navy jet aerobatics team is to perform Saturday and Sunday at the Dallas Naval Air Station's air show.

So this Navy public affairs officer was calling to confirm the flight. Then another Navy publicist called later. "You might not want to eat anything before you come out," he said. "Maybe just some bread to soak up the stomach juices."

Then still another called. "Don't drink any coffee or acidic juices, but you can eat a light lunch of bland food."

I'll say one thing for these Navy folks: They know how to generate excitement.

Finally, the appointed day arrived for me to fly the highway to the bland food zone. I got out to the Naval Air Station just as the Blue Angels' first passenger of the day was returning—a rugged-looking guy called "Hollywood" who flies KEGL's "Black Thunder" traffic helicopter.

"Did you black out?" someone asked him. "Yeah, once,' he said. "In a tight turn."

Blacked out? No one had mentioned that possibility. I thought my only worry was an upset tummy.

Jamie Aitken from "8 Country Reporter" took the next ride. He returned 30 minutes later looking exhilarated and a little green.

I forgot to ask if he had lapsed into any comas along the way.
Now it was my turn. I put on a snazzy flight suit with lots of pockets and zippers.

I looked quite dashing, I must say. Like a cross between Tom Cruise and Eddie Rickenbacker.

Crew chief Don Strahan had already briefed me, stressing how to avoid unconsciousness when undergoing extreme G-forces in the jet. "You want to stop the blood from rushing out of your head," he said.

"You do that by tightening every muscle in your body, especially in your abdomen. You push like you were having a baby," he said. "Or going to the bathroom," he whispered.

Then I signed a form saying I wouldn't be mad at the Navy if I died.

I met the pilot, Lt. Matt Seamon, a handsome fellow with a square jaw, a friendly smile and an even better flight suit than mine.

With Don's help, I strapped into the rear seat of the beautiful F-18. Ankle straps, knee straps, lap straps, shoulder straps. Much like an electric chair. He pointed out the seat ejection handle. He urged that I not touch it.

Matt strapped in, and soon we were rocketing down the runway. At least I thought we were rocketing—until he kicked in the afterburner. It nailed me to the seat. Warp speed.

We had been instructed to climb to 4,000 feet. Just for fun, Matt said we would try to hit 4,000 feet before clearing the end of the runway. We shot straight up. The altimeter quickly said 4,000, and Matt snapped the plane over on its side. Sure enough, there was the tire-blackened runway still beneath us.

We zipped toward Waco at better than 600 miles an hour, then began a series of aerobatic maneuvers. How did it feel? Sort of like riding one of those high-performance racing motorcycles. Over a cliff.

I was so disoriented most of the time that I wasn't sure whether we were looping, rolling or dying.

Don't tell the taxpayers, but I even got to briefly take the control stick of this $28 million flying federal investment. Bank right. Bank left. A few quick rolls. Hey, piece of cake.

Next, Matt flew some blood-rushing high-gravity turns. Each time I grunted a little harder against the G-forces.

On the last one, I was giving birth to triplets when the next thing I heard was Matt saying, "Are you back with me?"

"Yeah," I said weakly. He said, "You were only out for about a second."

By the time we got back on the ground, I was in a cold sweat with possibly the world's first fatal case of motion sickness.

"You're good at this," Matt insisted. "You handled those G's real well."

Of course, I did. I slept through them.

October 20, 1989

It's not just a walk;
it's an adventure

IT WAS SUCH a pretty day on Monday, I decided to walk to work. All 16 miles.

The idea had been on my mind for a long time. I wish someone had slapped me.

Actually, the walk started well and ended well. It was just the middle part that made me pray for a miracle—in the form of a cab.

It's an odd feeling to walk out your front door and down the driveway and just keep going.

It was nice, though. Something about walking heightens your senses. Or maybe cars just dull them. Have you ever noticed how many birds there are? And all that chirping!

But pedestrians are clearly not part of the suburban plan. Many streets had no sidewalks, not even footpaths worn in the weeds.

An hour after leaving my home in Sunnyvale, I crossed over LBJ and into the miserable phase. The quiet residential streets meandered in directions I didn't want to go. The major streets were a nightmare of noise and speed and fumes.

The invention of cars did more than make walking unnecessary. They also made it unpleasant.

At one point, I ended up walking along the service road of R.L. Thornton Freeway. A bombing raid in Baghdad would have been more pleasant.

I cut over to Samuell Boulevard. But the gravel shoulders made walking difficult. I felt sore spots rising on my feet.

They say you can't go for a walk in small towns because so many people stop to offer you a ride.

Dallas is not a small town.

At Jim Miller Road, the aroma from Big Al's Smokehouse reeled me in. And that was the turning point of the trip. The restorative powers of chopped beef and iced tea are amazing.

The air actually felt cool as I started out again. I took a detour through Grove Hill cemetery and peeked in the windows of the creepy, old mausoleums.

Further down Samuell, where the liquor stores are clustered, a teen-aged boy called me over. He was standing beside a gray Cutlass.

"These girls want to ask you something," he said.

The two girls inside and the boy appeared to be about 16. Sheepishly, the girl sitting behind the wheel asked, "Could you go in there and get us some wine coolers?"

They looked like good kids out on a spring lark. I could identify. But my "dad" instincts ran stronger.

"Naw, I'd better not," I said, feeling as sheepish as the kids. I couldn't disapprove too much. I remembered doing the very same thing.

I was walking on the park side of the street 10 or 15 minutes later when the same kids passed by and pulled into a convenience store lot. They beckoned to a man standing out front.

I leaned against a fence and watched. They talked a good while, then the man went into the store. Jackpot. He came out carrying a big grocery bag stacked full of wine coolers.

The kids pulled in their haul and zoomed out, headed east. And to what future? I wondered.

From there the walk was a piece of cake. East Dallas is made for walking, and the mix of humanity is rich and yeasty.

On Gurley Avenue, a Hare Krishna in saffron robes tugged at a loaded dolly.

A weather-beaten old man sat on his haunches outside a neighborhood grocery. "Say, son, you got a quarter I could have?" It was apparently my day to buy alcohol.

I passed on into Deep Ellum. At United Paper Recycling, I noticed the quote board with prices being paid for scrap paper.

Newspapers were fetching 25 cents per 100 pounds. Corrugated paper brought $1.

It's nice to know your work would be worth more if it were printed on the side of a box.

I got into the heart of downtown about 4 p.m., just as many people were starting for home. I had been walking for 6 1/2 hours.

There is a certain satisfaction in simple tasks—sweeping a floor, weeding a flower bed. And so it was with my walk.

I arrived at the office feeling vaguely like I had accomplished something—besides blisters.

May 8, 1991

Discovering treasures
in Sierra Madre

REAL DE CATORCE, Mexico—We had been in Mexico only about 10 seconds before a policeman was screaming at us.

You might say it was a shaky start.

My family and I were beginning a little driving tour through Mexico. I've always heard you shouldn't do that—which, naturally, always made me want to do it.

Let me say right here at the start that the guidebooks are wrong about one thing. You don't need Spanish, they say. Plenty of people speak English, they say.

In the resorts maybe. But try telling that to the border crossing guard in Nuevo Laredo.

With my limited Spanish, I thought he was telling us to proceed. But apparently he was telling us to proceed only as far as the inspection area just ahead.

When I drove past it, bells started ringing and lights flashed and a uniformed officer came running after us, waving one of those big clublike flashlights and screaming something.

I couldn't understand what he was saying, but I don't think it was "Bienvenidos a Mexico."

I was forced to make a big U-turn right there in the busy intersection while a group of amused fellows watched from the sidewalk. What's the Spanish word for "embarrassing"?

The inspection itself was quick and painless. But my wife and daughter were already reaching for the Tums.

The next stop was the immigration office, where we had to get tourist cards and a permit for the car. That took about an hour and more muddled Spanglish conversations.

As we waited, I noticed lots of other cars with U.S. plates. But all the other people appeared to be Latinos—who knew what they were doing.

It looked like we were the only family of suburban gringo yuppie scum headed into Mexico that morning.

Finally, we headed out. And as we drove through Nuevo Laredo, my son asked sincerely, "Did Mexico used to be pretty?"

Ah, my little Ugly American.

The truth is that the border area was pretty dismal—and that's probably what scares many visitors from venturing any farther.

But soon Nuevo Laredo was behind us and the Sierra Madre were rising in front of us, and we remembered why we came.

The contrasts of Mexico struck us immediately. Coming into Monterrey, a modern airport with rows of gleaming private planes was on our right. On our left, a peasant plodded along the highway in a horse-drawn wagon.

In the middle of Monterrey, familiar signs were all around—Wal-Mart, Blockbuster, 7-Eleven. But at a stoplight, a man stood at my window, fervently trying to sell us fresh ears of corn still in the shuck.

"Call me crazy," Allison said, "but I don't think we're in America anymore."

The driving was just fine. The highways are rougher than ours. But drivers aren't nearly as wild as rumored. In fact, everyone has been nice and courteous. And not a single bandito in the bunch.

I made a strategic error, however, in picking our first destination. I probably should have picked a nice Holiday Inn as our first stop.

Instead, I chose Real de Catorce—a real-life ghost town west of Mahtehuala. It boomed as a silver mining city in the 1700s and 1800s but has only a few hundred residents now.

To get there, we had to drive 30 miles off the main highway. Then turn off that road onto a 17-mile bladder-busting cobblestone road. That led us up into the mountains to a crude, one-lane tunnel almost two miles long. It was weird. And spooky.

When we came out of the tunnel, we entered Real de Catorce—the strangest place I have ever seen. It felt like a lost city, where people live among the ruins of an ancient civilization.

Goats and burros wandered the narrow streets. And our hotel was an odd place, clean but rustic, perched on the side of the mountain next to the cemetery.

Allison said it exactly: "I feel like I'm on another planet."

I think we all experienced the true definition of "culture shock." In the midst of all this splendid squalor, Corey said earnestly, "I sure appreciate America now."

That alone was probably worth making the trip. But I hope by week's end he's appreciating Mexico, too.

June 8, 1994

Family falls under
spell of San Miguel

SAN MIGUEL de ALLENDE, Mexico—When last we left the Blow family in Mexico, they were in culture shock, bordering on a culture coma.

Now, let me tell you about the place that snapped us back to life –San Miguel de Allende.

I'm telling you, it's magical. It's like a little slice of Europe—but without the French.

Of course, the rap on this place among Mexico purists is that there are too many Americans here. San Miguel de Chicago, they call it.

Well, add four more Americans under the spell of San Miguel.

I don't know that we'll ever move here, like so many Americans do, but the place is a bona fide treasure.

San Miguel is about 160 miles northwest of Mexico City. And once again, the drive here was smooth and easy.

I almost hate to say that. It seems so anticlimactic. After all the horror stories about driving in Mexico, I feel like a real failure for having no harrowing tales to report.

We did manage to get ourselves good and lost in the crowded streets of Matehuala. That produced a few anxious minutes. But we asked a police officer for directions, and though we didn't understand a word, her hand motions were good enough to get us back to the highway.

And now that I think about it, there was one shocking incident. We stopped for lunch at a nice little highway cafe. I ordered chicken tacos, and they came rolled like enchiladas! With French fries on top!

I must say, these Mexicans have a lot to learn about Mexican food. Their dishes are far too varied and interesting to qualify as Tex-Mex. Not once have I found a chili-drenched Combo Dinner No. 1 on the menu.

We were so hungry for home cooking that when we got to San Miguel, we made our way to a restaurant called Mexas—that's Tex-Mex from the southern perspective.

It was wonderful—fajitas, chimichangas, margaritas. Just like home.

Maybe that's the charm of San Miguel. It feels like home so quickly. This gracious, oh-so-civilized city makes those Mexican horror stories seem laughable.

"That's really a crock, isn't it?" Clyde Sharpe said over breakfast one morning. The retired businessman and his wife, Ally, were staying in our hotel during a five-week driving trip through Mexico.

"I feel safer here than I would in downtown Dallas, that's for sure."

The Sharpes, who divide their time between homes in Oklahoma City and South Padre Island, have been driving through Mexico since the 1950s. "In all that time, we have never been in any situation where I felt any fear," Clyde said.

Our hotel, La Mansion del Bosque, is a wonderful old place, by the way. We sat out in the lush courtyard in the evening, listening to the church bells on the town plaza and children's laughter in nearby Benito Juarez Park.

Ruth Hyba, formerly of Memphis, owns the place. She was among the first wave of American immigrants to arrive in San Miguel in the 1950s.

These days there are a few too many Americans in residence for her taste. You know how it is with those immigrants—they come flooding in, jabbering in their own language, playing their own music, taking over whole neighborhoods . . . sound familiar?

Admittedly, the American influence does dilute the foreign flavor a bit. A bumper sticker seen near the historic town plaza: "I'm an Aggie's Mom."

As a city established by Spanish colonists in 1542, San Miguel is full of beauty and culture and history. But here's what really sold my family on this place—the shopping.

We were lucky enough to be here on a special market day. It was Canton's First Monday Trades Day and Cinco de Mayo rolled into one. Vendors hawked their goods. Women sat on the ground slicing the pricklies off edible prickly pears. And nifty T-shirts sold for $6.

Earlier in the trip, my wife had admired the large mugs that our coffee was served in at breakfast. She was thrilled to spot them at a market in San Miguel.

And I wish you could have seen Lori's face when the clerk announced the price. Dos pesos—about 65 cents.

Culture shock? What culture shock? Viva Mexico!

June 10, 1994

Mexico trip's been a pleasure, but it's time to come home

TAMAZUNCHALE, Mexico—It's not as hard as it looks. Just say "Thomas and Charlie."

Our stay here in "Thomas and Charlie" has been great. But old "Steve and Lori" are definitely ready to head for home.

"Allison and Corey" were ready a couple of days ago.

Believe me, it's nothing against Mexico. The trip has been a pleasure— and an adventure.

It's just that we're ready to be back among the familiar—things like smooth roads, fast food and soft beds (mine, in particular).

I don't know if a single trip can prove much of anything, but all the hand-wringing over Mexican travel sure seems silly now.

I hate to keep sounding so darn cheery, but the drive over here from San Miguel de Allende was another breeze.

We drove eastward from San Miguel through some of the most spectacular mountain scenery I have ever seen.

Oh darn, here's another piece of good news—none of us got the dreaded *turista* stomach bug. But the twisting and turning on that narrow mountain road gave Allison a major case of car sick-erista.

We spent the night in a monastery-turned-hotel in the little town of Jalpan. And the color slowly returned to Ali's face.

The next day we drove on to Tamazunchale. I should say "tropical" Tamazunchale.

Bananas and mangos grow along the highway here. And coffee beans and oranges grow on the steep hillsides.

This was a stop recommended by "Mexico Mike" Nelson, the free-wheeling character who charts the roads of Mexico for Sanborn's Insurance travel guides. It's not really a conventional tourist stop, but he likes the people here, and I can see why.

In contrast to that bandito nonsense, the people in Tamazunchale are warm and hospitable. And they would love more visitors.

One of the local English teachers, Rudolfo Jonguitud (we just called him "Rudy"), heard we were in town and took us on a wonderful tour of the area.

We drove out into the countryside to a place where those high-priced tropical plants we buy in Dallas just spring from the ground—

ferns, crotons, palms, dracena and ficus. The air was filled with butterflies, and the trees were covered with wild red orchids.

Corey made friends with the son of the hotel owner, and the two 14-year-olds were soon off roaming the town, playing video games and doing the things 14-year-old boys do—apparently unhampered by lack of a common language.

The hotel here is new and beautiful—Hotel Tamazunchale. Corey was in heaven. The room had a TV—our first in Mexico. With ESPN!

Prices in Mexico are about like those in the United States. This room was $57. Gas is a little higher. Food is a little cheaper. You can find some bargains, but don't come to Mexico expecting poverty prices.

It's been a fascinating week. I think it was Texas that used the tourism slogan "Land of Contrasts." But believe me, it can't compare to Mexico—Land of Surrealistic Contrasts.

This country somehow manages to live in two centuries. In Mexico, pigs still wander the streets and satellite dishes sit atop the smallest hut.

I have to say that driving in Mexico is not for the faint-hearted.

My heart almost fainted several times. Like the time we came around a curve on a mountain highway and there was a huge truck coming from the other lane and a couple of cows standing in ours.

I hit the brakes and managed to miss a cow's nose by a nose.

In Mexico, we found you're in far more danger from burros on the highway than banditos.

Somehow we managed to miss all the bad stuff that supposedly happens here. We didn't get robbed. We didn't get thrown in jail. We never ran out of gas. We didn't get sick. No one asked us for a bribe.

We just don't know how to have fun.

Undoubtedly bad things must sometimes befall visitors here— just like in the United States.

But I think we've done a real disservice to Mexico by clinging to some old notions about its honesty and safety.

And in the process, we've only succeeded in cheating ourselves out of some wonderful travel experiences.

Our week in Mexico was travel of the best sort. We're headed back with new appreciation for another country—and new gratitude for home.

June 12, 1994

I dropped,
I plopped... I lived

SO AS I was crawling out of the airplane, 11,000 feet above the Terrell Municipal Airport, I distinctly heard me ask myself, "Are you really doing this?"

I didn't answer, but kept on crawling—grabbing the wing strut, balancing one foot on the little step outside the door, dangling the other foot in the air, trying not to think too plainly about leaping toward the Earth two miles below with only folded fabric on my back.

Once in position, I looked left and right at the jumpmasters who would be going out alongside me. Each gave a nod. "Ready," I hollered. "Set . . . ."

But before we go, a word of explanation. See, I had made a single parachute jump 20 years ago. And when it was over, and I was ready to pat myself on the back for incredible bravery, the instructor sneered that everyone goes through with the first jump.

"It's the second jump that takes guts," he said.

So . . . . Twenty years later . . . . "Ready," I hollered. "Set . . . ." And already I had goofed up.

I was supposed to rock backward on "ready," setting the rhythm for all three of us to jump smoothly together. Instead, I rocked forward. "Se . . . (crud) . . . et," I hollered, with a jerky catch-up motion. "Go . . . !"

OK, now another little problem. See, I was supposed to shove off into a big face-down, spread-eagle position with shoulders thrown back in a "hard arch." That's what keeps you stable in the air.

I, on the other hand, immediately went spinning backward, out of control—sky, ground, sky, ground, EEEIIII!

Before I had time to wet my pants—a jaunty blue jumpsuit, actually—my hard arching finally worked and I found myself ripping toward Earth in a nice, stable position.

They call it free fall, but you really don't have much free time. I had a whole laundry list of little drills to do. Mostly they want to see if your mind will work in midair, I think.

Everything just felt fast, very fast. We were plummeting downward at 120 miles an hour, and the roar was tremendous.

It really felt more like flying than falling, but the altimeter on my chest told me otherwise.

At 5,500 feet, I flashed "5-5" with my fingers, letting the jumpmasters know that I was aware of my altitude and would pull the rip cord at 5,000 feet.

I looked at the altimeter again, and it was time. "Look . . . Reach . . . Pull!"

With a wonderful, wonderful jolt, the parachute snapped open. In an instant, I went from blasting through the sky to quietly floating on air. I quickly looked up to inspect the canopy for "bag lock" or "slider-up snivel" or any of a dozen possible malfunctions.

It looked perfect.

I didn't know that I had been especially worried, but I found myself dangling up there in the air with a mile-wide grin on my face, actually yelling toward that beautiful canopy, "Yes! Yes! YES!!!"

There's nothing quite as exhilarating as not dying.

The canopy ride was the best part. A low-tech form of flying. I pulled on the toggle lines above my head, steering the parachute back and forth and around.

After free falling 6,000 feet in 35 seconds, the four minutes under the parachute seemed like slow motion. I loved it.

And I must say, I did an excellent job of judging the wind and hitting the landing area. But I goofed up at the last minute and flared the parachute too soon.

Instead of bringing it to a stop just as I touched the ground, it stopped while I was still about five feet up. I plopped to the ground like a sack of potatoes.

A happy sack of potatoes.

Back at the hangar, jumpmaster Bill Schmitt discussed my mistakes, then congratulated me on a successful jump. Feeling proud, I asked him if a lot of people really do chicken out on their second jump.

"Nah," he said. "It's usually the third or fourth jump. They just lose confidence."

The third or fourth jump? Argh!

October 1, 1995

What we won't do
for our kids

SO THERE I stood along the track of the Texas Motor
Speedway, waiting to drive a real NASCAR race car. And realizing that I
had made a serious strategic error.

I had forked over $325 last weekend to attend the Team Texas
High Performance Driving School. And now I was about to take my
eight laps around the speedway.

During the classroom part, chief instructor Mike Starr had asked
us to put our egos away and drive the cars at whatever speed felt
comfortable. "The cars can run up to 6,000 RPMs—about 150 miles per
hour," he had said. "But very few drivers will actually hit 6,000 RPMs
today."

Four cars run on the track at a time, he said, and there's no
shame in being passed.

That all sounded good. But as I prepared to drive, I realized I had
made a serious error: I had brought my 17-year-old son along.

And I knew that if I got out there on that track and poked around,
getting passed by other drivers, I would forever disgrace myself in
Corey's eyes. And whether fathers want to admit it or not, the approval
we crave most is from our own sons.

On top of that, my family has lately begun to accuse me of
"driving like a grandpa." That's because I stop at yellow lights and
generally find the speed limit about right. But maybe, down deep, I was
starting to question my own reflexes.

Then it was my turn. And let me tell you, the first real test of
ability was climbing into the car through that little side window. Creak.
Groan. Stretch.

I wiggled in and got a surprise. The steering wheel was lying up
on the dash. Hmm, hope they fix that.

I introduced myself to my passenger, instructor Ken Mosbey,
who must surely be one of the bravest men in the world. With a lot of
help from the pit crew, my harness was hooked up, the steering wheel
was attached (always a good idea), and I pulled on my helmet.

"Open the throttle just a little," one of the pit guys said. He
reached in and flipped a switch. The engine roared to life. And I felt like
I was in the belly of a beast. A screaming, trembling 600-horsepower
tiger.

Here we go. I was in sort of a dreamlike state. First gear. Pop the clutch. Lurching start. Oops, bad form.

Down pit row. Second gear. Now out onto the inside apron of the track. Engine screaming. Third gear. Around Turn 2. Now fourth gear. Out onto the back straightaway. And PUNCH IT!

Wheee! Yiiii!

I cruised around that first lap nice and easy. Ken reached over a few times to tug the steering wheel and help me find the proper "line" on the track.

Then he gave me the thumbs up. Let 'er rip. And off I went. I just took it on faith that the car would stay on the track in the turns. Because it felt like I was going far faster than physics would allow.

I had no idea how fast I was going. But for Corey's sake, I knew I was pushing it.

Suddenly one of the other cars appeared in front me. Coming out of Turn 2, I nailed it and passed him low on the back straightaway. I felt like apologizing as I roared by. "I'm doing it for my so-o-o-on!"

It was all a blur. And a blast. Hug the wall. Now swoop down through a turn. Release pressure on the wheel and fly back out to the wall. Ken put out a flat hand, telling me to hold that speed.

Now another car was in front of me. In class they had said to pass only on the back straightaway, but Ken gave me a sign and I ripped around that car on the outside of a turn.

Corey, I thought, you better be watching this!

Just as I was getting comfortable—and probably dangerous—the checkered flag told me my eight laps were done.

I coasted into pit row with the engine off, and Ken patted me on the shoulder. "Good job," he said.

Maybe he says that to all the drivers. But it felt better than a victory lap to me.

As I unhooked all the harness straps, Ken flipped a switch to check how high the tach had gone during the run. 6,000 RPMs! 150 miles an hour. I had done it!

I climbed out and looked toward Corey. He gave me a little grin.

Yeah, call me "grandpa" now.

July 20, 1997

Down under, with
tanks to Mike Nelson

LET'S CALL it my tribute to Lloyd Bridges.

Like a lot of kids, I grew up watching "Sea Hunt." Actually, I grew up worshiping "Sea Hunt."

I wanted to be Mike Nelson. Every summer was spent splashing around in Lake Tyler or Fun Forest swimming pool with my $5 flippers and goggles.

Well, now I know the real things are called "fins" and "mask." What's the difference? About $200.

Yes, I'm taking scuba lessons. At 45, I'm still playing "Sea Hunt." And it's so cool.

We haven't even left the little training pool yet, and I love it.

Funny though, my childhood scuba fantasies never included having a teenage son along as a sidekick. But Corey wanted to join me in this little adventure. And I was glad to have him.

He did, however, scold me last week during class for wearing my weight belt too high. You know—fashion first.

We're taking lessons at our neighborhood dive shop, Aqua World in South Garland. The instructor is Karen Jones, who works by day as a stockroom manager for Texas Instruments.

She's very nice, but I can't say that of the assistant instructors. When I got choked on a mouthful of water the other day, one of them barked, "Don't drink from the pool."

Aw, actually they're all nice, very patient. We had to start our first pool session by swimming 20 laps. It's a small pool (indoor and heated), but I had just wolfed down two chili-cheese-onion hot dogs.

I felt like I was swimming with the parking brake on.

But no one made fun of me for finishing last. Except Corey.

I can't tell you how many times I imagined myself with all that cool scuba gear on, rolling backward into the water just like Mike Nelson always did.

Our actual start was a little less dramatic: We stood in the pool and put our faces in the water. Wheee!

It was like going back to water-baby swim lessons. But we were breathing underwater, by golly.

Unexpected first impression: Those bubbles are loud! They really rattle up around your ears. I distinctly remembered them murmuring softly on "Sea Hunt."

Before that first pool session was over, Karen had us all so comfortable underwater that we were removing our masks, replacing them and clearing the water out.

One disappointment: When we're on the surface, we're not allowed to push our masks up on our foreheads. Mike always did that on TV and looked very dashing. But in the water, it's a sign of a panicked diver. So it's a no-no—unless panicked.

Actually, I haven't panicked once. Breathing underwater feels far more natural than I expected. They did get my attention during class with the little phrase "lung rupture." But you can avoid that by "always, always breathing continuously while scuba diving and never, never holding your breath." (The first rule of scuba. I'm betting it will be on the final exam.)

We spend a lot of time practicing safety measures. And scuba really doesn't seem so risky now. Mike Nelson was always running out of air at the worst possible time—like with his legs pinned under a huge stack of falling pipes.

That hasn't happened once, so far.

But we have learned to always dive with a buddy and that modern scuba regulators (the hose thingy) have an extra mouthpiece just for sharing with a buddy.

There's just one problem—Corey is my buddy.

There's something unsettling about entrusting your life to a 17-year-old male.

Of course, Corey insists that I'll be the problem in an emergency. I chided him for not reading all materials thoroughly. And he shot back, "Oh, sure. If I was drowning, you'd be over there reading off "the side of your tank: 'Hmm, this was made in China . . .' "

OK, I'm guilty of reading carefully. My buddy, on the other hand, speed reads everything but talks at length of "sticking stuff" with his dive knife.

Well, we have have one more week of lessons to survive. Then, next weekend, we go to Lake Travis near Austin for our final check-out dives.

I'll let you know if we pass—or flail.

April 12, 1998

Scuba novice
encounters new depths

LAKE TRAVIS, Texas—The scuba lessons back in Dallas had gone so well.

Up until the last little exercise, that is.

For that one, the instructors took our masks, flipped them out into the 12-foot end of the pool and said, "Go find yours."

Well, something about scuba diving without a mask and scrambling among my classmates down there on the bottom left me feeling kind of flustered. I swam to the surface and caught my breath.

It was no big deal. I quickly went back down to complete the exercise. We all sat on the bottom and traded masks around to practice clearing flooded masks underwater.

It was no big deal. And yet . . . .

My son and I arrived at Scuba Park on Lake Travis early Saturday for two days of check-out dives and a night of camping. In addition to all the gear packed in the back of the van, I also carried a seed of self-doubt lodged in the back of my mind.

But I pushed it aside and plunged ahead. After years of watching "Sea Hunt" reruns, my moment to really scuba dive was finally at hand.

Let me tell you, the first big hurdle was putting on that skin-tight wet suit. The folks on TV and in the movies always look so dashing in them. But they never show anyone actually putting on a wet suit, do they?

It's not a pretty sight. We're talking head-to-toe girdle. Imagine a sausage putting itself into a casing.

I squeezed into the pants, jacket, boots, gloves and hood—and could barely breathe on land. I didn't know how I was going to do it underwater.

But the first dive went well. Two at a time we descended to a metal platform on the bottom, 40 feet down. We repeated some of the exercises we had practiced in the pool, then went for a swim.

It was really a strange sensation down there. Kind of cold and creepy. But enthralling, too. Big perch circled curiously around us. Some swam right up to my mask. It occurred to me that I'd never been eyeball to eyeball with a fish in its own territory.

Then came the second dive of the day. For some reason, I didn't descend smoothly this time. I flailed around, trying to stay positioned in the water, watching, watching for the bottom to come into view. By the time I got there, I was gasping for air through my regulator. It felt like I was suffocating.

I signaled to instructor Karen Jones that I wanted to go back up. She grabbed my harness straps and gave me an emphatic "no" shake of the head.

I knew what I was supposed to do—relax and take deep breaths. Yeah, well try that in a sausage suit 40 feet underwater. But finally, slowly, my breathing began to even out.

Then it was time for the first exercise. I was to half-fill my mask with water, then blow through my nose to clear it.

Well, that water surged into my mask, I snorted a little through my nose and went into a choking fit. Again, Karen held me down, telling me with her gestures to work through it.

But I couldn't. I gasped and coughed through the mouthpiece. Every hacking gasp grew shorter. I couldn't catch my breath. And I wanted up NOW!

I bolted for the surface. Gasping every inch of the 40 feet and unsure I would make it.

But I did. It was not a pretty picture—gasping, gagging, belching. And loud sighs of terror and relief.

Then Karen said, "OK, let's go back down and try it again."

Uh, no thank you. At that moment I could barely bring myself to put my head underwater, much less return to the bottom.

I got out, took off all the gear, rested a bit and talked to myself a lot. My strong instinct was to quit right there. Hey, "Sea Hunt" was always kind of corny, if you really think about it.

I wondered if my son would forgive me if I quit. I wondered if my wife would forgive me if I died.

And I was really embarrassed and mad at myself. I had secretly prided myself on doing so well in the classes. Now I had this image of my classmates standing over my drowned body, saying, "Gosh, he only missed one on the written test."

Come back next time and I'll tell you the finish.

April 22, 1998

Building up the courage
to take the plunge

LAKE TRAVIS, Texas—So there I sat on the dock, short of breath—and courage.

If you've been following my "Sea Hunt" saga, you know that my son and I have been taking scuba lessons. We went to Lake Travis last weekend for our final checkout dives.

And if you caught the previous episode—"Smothered Chicken"—you know that things didn't go swimmingly on my second dive.

Forty feet down, I suddenly felt like I was suffocating. Bad enough. But then came the first exercise—flooding the mask with water and clearing it.

Well, I choked. In every sense.

In a gagging, gasping fit, I clawed my way to the surface. And if my Christian faith had been stronger, I would have walked back to the dock.

Instead, I shakily swam back, got out and pondered quitting.

I'll confess that I thought of you. Could I write a column about chickening out of scuba school? Yes, I could, I decided.

Other divers on the dock were nice. They told me about their setbacks and encouraged me to try again.

But it was my 17-year-old son who made me go on. At the moment, Corey was out there underwater, going through his exercises. And I really wanted us to have this bond of scuba diving.

So I went back.

More nervous than anything since seventh-grade P.E., I sank those 40 long feet back to bottom. When instructor Karen Jones gave the sign, I pulled the mask from my face and felt water rush in.

I closed my eyes and concentrated on breathing through my mouth. Then I exhaled sharply through my nose and opened my eyes to find the mask clear.

I wasn't dead! Karen gave me a high five and we finished the dive.

I was hugely relieved. But I wasn't done yet. I had two more the next day. And I knew I had to flood my mask again for the third dive and remove it completely for the fourth dive.

It was a sleepless night. While Corey slumbered blissfully beside me, I fretted about those next two dives.

Corey hadn't been much help when I confessed my stress. "Grown-ups think too much," he muttered. Yeah, that's how we survived to be grown-ups.

One of the dive masters had made me feel good. In a private moment, Vern Applegate said he had never seen a student go back down after an episode like mine. "That took a lot of guts," he said.

But did I have enough to do it again?

I hadn't expected scuba to provide a major life lesson. I was just playing Mike Nelson. But I learned a lot about the paralyzing power of self-doubt. I had done these exercises in the pool without a hitch. But now, with a pinch of doubt, my heart pounded at the thought of them.

Classmates Carol Orkis and Scarlett Clark were the ones who had joked about nervousness during the lessons. Now they were breezing through, along with Scarlett's son, Josh. And I was the one still thinking of quitting.

Finally morning came. And more from stubbornness than courage, I plunged ahead. Vern was assigned as my dive buddy. He didn't say a word about the previous day, but I knew he was pulling for me.

Well, it wasn't the prettiest mask flood ever performed. But I got through it. And I almost enjoyed the rest of the dive as we swam around sunken boats.

Then came the last dive and the mask removal exercise. For the first time, I was diving in a group with Corey. I watched as he nonchalantly popped the mask off his face, pushed his swirling hair back and replaced the mask. Piece of cake.

Karen turned to me and I didn't give myself time to think. I pulled the mask off, and somewhat to my surprise, my breaths kept coming, smooth and easy.

I loved scuba! Suddenly I was Mike Nelson again. With all the exercises done, Vern and I swam off together and fed wieners to a herd of 50-pound catfish that lumbered around us.

We got back to the dock and everyone congratulated me. I was a certified diver. And I felt incredibly happy.

They all said I would enjoy it even more when the water is nice and warm. But to really write about scuba, they said, you have to go to Cozumel.

Hmmm . . . . Cozumel. Magical words began to play across my mind—warm water, crystal clear, expense account . . . .

April 24, 1998

TV Preachers, 'Babatists' & Other Fellow Sinners

HONESTLY, I never intended to make a crusade of picking on TV preachers. But once you begin to watch them, how can you stay silent? Lordy, what a crew! I wrote far more about ol' Robert Tilton than I ever expected, but every column seemed to lead to another more outlandish one.

For that matter, I never intended to write about religion as much as I have. But the one promise that I made to myself when I began the column was that I was just going to be myself. My faith is important to me. Religion fascinates me. So I have felt drawn to the topic often.

My fellow Southern Baptists have certainly provided lots to discuss over the last few years. The "Sermon On the Mouse" was probably one of the most talked-about columns that I have ever written. And a few Southern Baptists still aren't talking to me!

Actually, I've gotten far more whispered "attaboys" from fellow Baptists than I have criticism. And while I sure don't hold myself out as a poster boy for Christianity, I hope my columns have made people more comfortable talking openly about spiritual issues.

The great loan officer in the sky

ONE OF THE fastest-growing TV ministries in recent years has been that of Dallas' own Robert Tilton.

Locally, he's known as pastor of the Word of Faith Church. But around the country, he's known as the charismatic preacher on the daily TV program Success-N-Life.

I thought it would be interesting to talk to the Rev. Tilton, so I called the church. "I'm sorry. He doesn't do interviews," a secretary said.

"Never?' I asked.

"No, never," she said.

I asked if someone else on the staff could speak for the ministry. "No, sir. Sorry. I'm afraid not," she said.

I asked if she could send me some written information. "No," she said. Finally I asked for any suggestion. "You could watch the program," she said.

And so I did. Here is some of what I learned. The Rev. Tilton speaks in tongues, casts out demons and cures the sick. But most of all, he preaches prosperity.

"See, I believe that God has anointed me to break the yoke of lack, the bondage of lack," he said. "You thought it was impossible, that you would never get ahead of the bills. But I hear the sound of abundance for you, say-eth the Lord."

This is how his Miracle Plan works: You give money to God (through Robert Tilton Ministries), and God gives you greater riches in return.

I learned that God often speaks directly to the Rev. Tilton. "God gave me this truth. He said, 'Bob, those that bless you in the work, I will bless them.' "

I learned that we can be quite specific in ordering our blessings. "I see a person right now. You've had a hard time with transportation. If you'll act out right now and seed for that car, God will cause that car to be a reality in your life.

"And I don't care what the creditors have said. You decide on what kind of a car you need for your family. You decide what size, what seats, two-door, four-door. You decide . . . and you seed for it. That seed will come up."

As for the size of the seed, the Rev. Tilton likes for people to pledge $1,000. "You say, 'Why make a thousand-dollar vow?' It's a vow of faith. Just pay on it every week. Maybe it will take a month to pay it. You may pay it immediately."

For some, $1,000 isn't enough. "There's a business person watching me right now. You need to make a $10,000 vow, then sit down and write out a check for all of it."

For some, anything less than $1,000 is too little. "Here is a $100 vow from Kalamazoo. OK, if that's where your level of faith is . . ."

But then the Rev. Tilton stopped himself. "No, Bonnie, you need to make a $1,000 vow of faith. There is something not right here. I've never said this on the air before, but Bonnie, something is wrong here. Nope." He set her pledge aside and prayed over the others.

I learned that it is dangerous not to obey. "If you don't tithe, I'll just tell you right now, there is a curse on your life."

The prosperity formula works for the Rev. Tilton's ministry, too. "You don't hear us on here crying the blues. Don't have to, because what I am preaching is working."

Yet he has no personal wealth, he said.

"See, I have nothing. I don't own any property. All I have, my wife and I have a couple of cars that we make payments on. We own no land. We own no houses. The whole organization and ministry owns our home. We don't have anything. . . ."

The Rev. Tilton not only talks with the Lord but wrestled with the devil. "The devil himself walked into my bedroom. He had come to kill me. I pray that never happens to you. And he was there because this ministry is helping so many people. He was mad because people who had been beat down into the slums and gutters of poverty and depression and defeat were being set free. . . . So pay on your vow today."

The Rev. Tilton's brand of Christianity seems almost nothing like what I've known. I grew up on a Christianity that talked of sacrifice and selflessness and offered a reward in the sweet by-and-by.

The Rev. Tilton's Christianity says there is no need to suffer, no need to wait. You can have it all in the here-and-now.

I don't know about his theology, but I admire his marketing.

March 11, 1990

Omnipresent? That's
neither here nor there

I NEED TO correct something in last Sunday's column about the Rev. Robert Tilton. I referred to the nationally broadcast TV minister as "Dallas' own."

Now I have learned that he belongs to San Diego more than Dallas.

Though his ministry is still based here, the Rev. Tilton and his family have apparently moved to an affluent area north of San Diego. But that's a secret we're not supposed to know.

His daily Success-N-Life TV show is now produced in studios near San Diego, but he commutes back to Dallas two or three Sundays a month to preach at his Word of Faith Family Church in Farmers Branch.

Last week I wrote about trying to interview the Rev. Tilton. A secretary told me no one in the ministry grants interviews. If I wanted further information, she said, I could watch the television program.

I did, but his TV show sure didn't tell me he was preaching from California. He repeatedly exhorts viewers to phone the Miracle Prayer Center in Dallas and make their $1,000 pledges of faith.

In fact, during the program, viewers periodically see "telephone counselors" receiving the calls. Then, toward the end of the show, someone off-camera hands the pledges to the Rev. Tilton so that he can pray over them. You certainly don't get the idea that the pledges are being handed from Texas to California.

But a news story last week in the *San Diego Tribune* detailed the Rev. Tilton's move to that area. The story quoted the Rev. Tilton's lawyer, J.C. Joyce of Tulsa, Okla., as saying the move was prompted by security concerns.

I called Mr. Joyce myself for more information. He said the move was necessary because a few years ago a Dallas newspaper—he didn't know which one—printed the address of the Tiltons' home. (They lived in Bent Tree.)

"The irresponsibility of the media in running someone's address in the paper is, well, all it did was drive them out of their residence,' Mr. Joyce said.

I asked if the Lord's work was really that dangerous. "He has received innumerable death threats," Mr. Joyce said.

He specifically cited an incident four years ago in which a human head was discovered in a restroom urinal at Word of Faith Family Church. "It would terrify any sane person," he said.

Detective Reece Daniel of the Farmers Branch Police Department investigated that case. Four teens were arrested. They had stolen the head from a mausoleum and apparently chosen the church at random, he said.

"They thought this was a way to make a splash and upset some people. They thought it was a great joke," Sgt. Daniel said. "I didn't see anything to indicate it was a personal threat."

Sgt. Daniel said he never heard any reports of threats against the Rev. Tilton.

Mr. Joyce said he can't explain why the Rev. Tilton would receive frequent death threats. "There are just a bunch of nuts out there. It's like the Hollywood celebrities who have had to go underground and hide from these nuts," he said.

Mr. Joyce confirmed that the Rev. Tilton now tapes his "Success-N-Life" program in studios near San Diego. But he refused to discuss where the Tiltons live. "Whether they live in Dallas or Boston, his personal residence is not going to be disclosed to anyone ever at any time if we can do anything about it."

In his story in the San Diego newspaper, reporter John Gilmore wrote, "Though it is unclear whether Tilton and his wife, Marte, and the couple's four children live here, their two 1988 dark blue Mercedes-Benzes are frequently parked outside the local office of Tilton's Word of Faith International in Sorrento Valley."

And he said that the Rev. Tilton lists his address as a post office box in the swank community of Rancho Santa Fe, located about 20 miles to the north.

I was still bothered by one thing, so I asked Mr. Joyce about it. On the TV show, how does the Rev. Tilton manage to pray over those offering pledges in San Diego if they are being phoned into the Miracle Prayer Center in Dallas?

"That's the beauty of a thing called fax,' Mr. Joyce said. "It's an amazing world we live in."

Amen to that, brother.

March 18, 1990

So much prosperity,
so little candor

RANCHO SANTA FE, Calif.—I hadn't had much luck trying to get an interview with the Rev. Robert Tilton, so I stopped by his house.

Of course that required a trip to California.

Brother Bob preaches at the Word of Faith Family Church in Farmers Branch, but the church parsonage is 1,100 miles away in an exclusive area north of San Diego.

It's supposed to be a big secret where Brother Bob lives. He moved from Dallas almost two years ago because he wanted more privacy and personal security, his lawyer said.

But secrets are hard to keep. Word spread quickly through the beautiful, high-security Fairbanks Ranch development that a mystery man was building the new home overlooking the lake—a man introducing himself only as "Bob."

It caused some alarm, residents said. Some thought "Bob" might be Mafia. Some guessed he was in the federal witness protection program.

But it wasn't long before "Bob's" identity was well known. After all, his daily "Success-N-Life" TV show is hard to miss. He buys time on 80-some-odd TV stations around the country, speaking in tongues, casting out demons and telling people that God will bless them with money and jobs and cars if they will just send in an offering.

Though he preaches a prosperity gospel, I once heard Brother Bob say on TV that he isn't wealthy. "See, I have nothing. I don't own any property. All I have, my wife and I have a couple of cars that we make payments on. We own no land. We own no houses. The whole organization and ministry owns our home. We don't have anything."

Well, let me tell you, we should all have so little.

Brother Bob lives in a gorgeous Mediterranean-style home. It's a six-bedroom, 7 1/2-bath house with 8,600 square feet. A swimming pool and guest house are located in back.

The house was purchased for $1.5 million in 1988, county records show. It was a good investment. It now may be worth as much as $4.5 million, said Brother Bob's lawyer, J.C. Joyce of Tulsa, Okla.

In fact, the house may soon go on the market. "The market is right to sell it," Mr. Joyce said. "It's a good prosperity story. That's the prosperity ministry."

I knocked on the big double doors, but darn the luck, Brother Bob wasn't home. Candis Darken was house-sitting. She was polite but a little frosty. I left a note asking Brother Bob to give me a call.

Just a few blocks from the house, waiting security guards stopped me and threatened me with trespassing charges for dropping in. Finally, though, they let me go with a courteous warning, in writing, that I would be arrested next time.

The next morning I stopped by Brother Bob's offices and TV studio, located not far from his home. The reception area was elegant, decorated in mauve and pale green. Photo portraits of Brother Bob hung on two walls.

His secretary, Roseann Rueffer, came out to tell me that Brother Bob does not grant interviews. And she said he wasn't in town anyway.

Roseann and I began to chat about the ministry. We sat in a couple of wing-backed chairs in the reception area and talked, off the record, for more than an hour. It was a nice visit. Suffice to say, she believes Brother Bob is a man of great integrity.

I told her that could very well be true, but that he operates his ministry in such secrecy that it's impossible for outsiders to make that judgment.

Word of Faith is run as though it were Brother Bob's private, multimillion-dollar corporation. There is no board of trustees, no deacons, no elders. He alone sets the policy. He alone sets the budget.

Brother Bob is "totally, completely and solely in control," Mr. Joyce said. I asked him how much Brother Bob pays himself. "None of your business," he said.

Mr. Joyce said Brother Bob makes no promises about how offerings will be spent, and therefore owes no explanation or accounting.

I do know one way the money is spent, however. While Ms. Rueffer and I sat talking about integrity and accountability, an office delivery arrived.

Word of Faith was blessed with two new paper shredders.

May 27, 1990

Bad taste is
couple's original sin

I'LL PROBABLY be sent straight to the devil for even bringing this up, but . . . . Have you seen Sister Jan Crouch?

Lordy, lordy, where does that woman shop?

I know we shouldn't judge people on their appearance. And I know that Christians aren't supposed to judge people, period.

So call this social commentary.

I can't help it. I'm fascinated by TV preachers. And the Trinity Broadcasting Network is now the world's largest religious network, with about 450 stations across America and around the globe.

Its founders are Paul and Jan Crouch, and they are almost hometown folks. That's their grand new International Production Center along Airport Freeway in Irving—the one that looks like the White House. And the Crouches spend much of their time at a ranch in Colleyville.

The couple host the network's nightly program, "Praise The Lord" (9 p.m. on KDTX-TV Channel 58 in Dallas, cable channel 19). You just have to see this production to appreciate it.

I'm not talking about content. It's the trappings. It's all that French froufrou furniture and gleaming chandeliers and brocade wallpaper. Paul tends to dress like a jaunty billionaire—that Thurston Howell the Third look. But it's Jan who is really over the top.

Her makeup must come in caulk guns. She has all this silvery purple hair piled up in big baby-doll swoops and curls. And then she completes the look with frilly, flouncy dresses.

The effect is sort of Tammy Faye Antoinette.

Look, I'm not the first person tacky enough to mention this. In fact, it's in Paul's own book, *I Had No Father But God*. In the foreword, California minister Jack W. Hayford talks about seeing the Crouches on TV before ever meeting them.

"Pardon my frankness . . . ," he wrote, "but as I gazed at the screen I was inwardly irritated. It wasn't anything that was said, it was simply that the Crouches didn't suit my taste. Everything seemed so 'overdone'—from their style, to the set, to Paul's suit and Jan's makeup."

The most vivid description of the Crouches may be from Ben Davis' hilarious and poignant book, *Strange Angel*. The late Mr. Davis was an Assemblies of God preacher from Dallas whose ministry took a detour when he realized he was gay.

Though he liked the Crouches, Mr. Davis wrote: "One major problem is Paul and Jan's total lack of taste in fashion and set design, which makes them come across as ignorant bumpkins. I'm sincere when I say I can't understand why Jan goes out of her way to make sure she looks like the madam of a Paris, Texas, whorehouse.

"That look is so totally opposite from the position of leadership she has, and it turns many people off to the Gospel. The woman simply should not be allowed to dress herself without adult supervision."

As for the set design, he wrote, "Its flaming red carpet, gaudy flocked wallpaper, Louis XIV furniture from Montgomery Ward, and drag queen staircase is a classic example of what can happen when straight people try to be interior decorators."

Broadcasts of "Praise The Lord" are open to the public, and I went Tuesday night just to see the spectacle for myself. It's even more eye-popping in person than on TV.

I was sorely disappointed that Jan wasn't there that night. But Paul did give due credit for the look of the place. "My little Jan has a pretty good little decorator's eye," he said.

Perhaps an eye patch is in order.

The irony is that I find myself liking the Crouches' program. They spend almost no time asking for money. And unlike other TV preachers these days, they use their time to lift up God rather than run down groups of people.

In the foreword to Paul's book, Dr. Hayford goes on to tell how God clearly and powerfully rebuked him for his judgmental attitude toward the Crouches.

I can't say I got the same divine kick in the pants Tuesday night. But I did leave the broadcast feeling that Paul Crouch is the real deal, a person of deep conviction—if not great fashion sense. I left feeling uplifted in spite of myself.

Paul and Jan may be the ultimate proof that God moves in mysterious ways. But he definitely moves.

September 9, 1994

Religious right's tack gives rise to misgivings

LIKE ALMOST everyone with an interest in politics and/or religion, I've been struggling to sort out my thoughts about the rise of the religious right.

To be more accurate, I guess I should say I have struggled to sort out my misgivings about this phenomenon.

Let me start with a few disclaimers. My distress has nothing to do with conservatism as a political philosophy. And neither do I quibble with Christians getting involved in issues of the day.

So what's my concern? Well, that's the hard part.

To begin, let me tell you a little bit about the church I grew up in. As I've said before, it was tiny. And old-timey, too.

We still observed something known as "foot-washing services," which will probably sound as bizarre as snake handling to many of you.

But it was a solemn ceremony for us—and particularly powerful for me as an adolescent boy coming to grips with grown-up spirituality.

The preacher would start with a little history lesson, about how folks in Bible days walked everywhere in open sandals and how they shared those dusty, dirty streets with camels and donkeys and goats.

It was a pretty vivid picture.

He would explain that when visitors entered a household, the lowliest servant would get the nasty job of washing the guests' feet.

Then the preacher would open the Gospel of John and read from the passage in which Jesus knelt at the feet of his disciples and, one by one, washed their feet in a dramatic demonstration of humility and forgiveness.

The preacher then would turn to other verses that make clear the awesome Christian contradiction—that we bring greatest glory to ourselves through the lowest servanthood to the poor and despised.

"For everyone who exalts himself will be humbled, and he who humbles himself will be exalted," says the Gospel of Luke.

Then we would rise from the pews, the men and women heading into separate rooms. (We certainly didn't believe in coed foot-washing in our church.)

Using shallow pans of water and small towels, we would take turns washing each other's feet. And I'm telling you, washing another fella's foot is an experience you don't soon forget.

For better or worse, that little church left me indelibly stamped with a certain view of Christianity. And I guess that's the heart of my misgivings today.

I have a hard time seeing humble servitude reflected in the religious right.

I don't know about you, but I can't see Jerry Falwell washing anybody's feet. Selling videotapes in the temple, maybe. But not kneeling to wash a Democratic tax-collector's feet.

I know that most conservative Christians have good, caring hearts. But I don't think their leaders have represented them well—or our faith.

When they talk about welfare reform, I don't get the idea that it's motivated by deep compassion for the poor. I hear contempt for welfare bums and cheats.

When they talk about Bill Clinton, I don't hear respectful disagreement with a Christian brother. I hear ridicule and a jumbo load of judgment.

When they talk about drug addicts and teen-age mothers and juvenile gangsters, I don't hear heartache for people caught in self-destructive ways. I hear disgust for those not playing by the rules of "traditional values."

Most critics of the religious right have worried about what these Christian politicians might do to democracy.

But my greatest concern is what these political Christians might do to Christianity.

I don't want my faith dragged down to the level of a quasi-political party. I don't want my spirituality turned into some politician's strange bedfellow.

Please, Christian Coalition, don't sell our faith short.

Government is ultimately about rules and regulations. Christianity is about a relationship.

Government is about changing behavior. Christianity is about changing the human heart.

To those outside the faith watching and wondering, I would simply say: Don't judge Christianity by all those who call themselves Christian. Me included.

If you wonder, open one of the Gospels and listen to the founder.

December 4, 1994

Pastor takes gritty
message to city streets

HE WORE A double-breasted, charcoal gray suit with a dark red tie and tasseled loafers.

He could have been just another executive walking along the streets of downtown Dallas.

Except that he wasn't walking. He was pacing the sidewalk, up and down, back and forth.

And he was preaching.

He cried out in a raspy, beseeching voice that echoed in the streets. He wasn't just preaching, he was pleading.

His Bible, laid atop a newspaper rack, identified him as the Rev. Melvin Brown of God's Tabernacle of Deliverance in Oak Cliff.

He preached in the black church style, giving his words a rhythm and a poetry that transcended the words themselves.

"We've got people turning to drugs to try to escape the reality of their situation," he cried out.

"Reality" came out like four words: "ree, al, uh, tee."

"But listen, mother," he said. "No matter how high you get"—pause—"when you come back down"—pause—"that baby is still going to be crying. Those bills are still going to be unpaid. Those burdens are still going to be on your shoulders."

Those waiting for buses—or simply waiting—at the corner of Elm and Ervay tried to pretend the preacher wasn't there.

But his words, gritty as any urban rapper's, reeled them in.

"You just got $800 in food stamps on Monday. On Tuesday you are knocking on your neighbor's door, asking for a cup of sugar. The dope man's got your food stamps.

"The dope man's got your TV. The dope man's got your VCR. The dope man's got your leather coat. The dope man's got your children's Nintendo."

An elderly woman stepped out into the center of the sidewalk, looking up Elm Street for her bus. She never looked at the preacher. But under her breath, she urged him on.

"Tell it," she said softly, finding the rhythm of his words. "Tell it."

"You go to church and you can't stay there two or three minutes," he said. "But you can stay two or three days in a rock house - as long as you've got the money to feed your habit.

"Dope has got you down so low you don't know what you're doing. You are scraping through the carpet, looking for something you know you did not drop. You are digging through the ashtray, looking for a doobie you know you did not put there.

"We've got mamas shootin' up. We've got daddies being shot down. We've got gangs banging on every corner. Blood is splattering on our sidewalks.

"We've got children living in filth and falling through the cracks. And you tell me we ain't got no problems. Brother, you may not like me, but you got to accept that what I'm saying is the truth."

A pause. Downshift in tone and tempo.

"No matter how lowdown a man or a woman is, I serve a God who can pick you up," he said. "God knows how to take those tears of pain and turn them into tears of joy. Hallelujah! God is able!

"The God I serve—I know he's able. You're looking at a three-time loser. One day, tracks all up and down my arm, my back against the wall, I came to Jesus. Thank you, Lord!

"That's what you've got to understand. God will accept us like he finds us. If he finds you with a needle in your arm . . . If he finds you slinging dust in the back of your nose . . . If he finds you in a red-light district on the wrong side of town . . . God will accept you right there.

"When Jesus got ready to find some disciples, he didn't go to Harvard University. He didn't go to SMU Law School. He went down to the projects. He went down to the fisherman at the seashore. He went into the West Dallas projects. He said: 'Drop your nets. Come follow me.'

"God is still taking zeroes and making heroes out of them. God is still taking prostitutes off the street and making them models in the church house. God can take a dope dealer and make a Baptist preacher out of him.

"You come from an orphan home? You don't know your mama or your daddy? Your subjects and your verbs may not agree. But God loves you. God accepts you.

"He loves you when you're up. He loves you when you're down. God looked past all my failures, and he saw my needs. Hallelujah!"

Another bus stopped. But some had already been transported.

April 7, 1995

The Rev. Blow gives
a sermon on the mouse

HALLELUJAH! Thank you Sister Jones for singing that wonderful special. Wasn't that a joyful noise?

I'm telling you, those high notes sent the Holy Spirit shooting through me like a bug zapper on a June bug.

Well, dear friends, welcome to another Wednesday prayer meeting here at the First Southern-Fried Self-Satisfied Babatist Church. I'm so fired up I just can't wait to start preachin'.

But before I get down to business, I just have to give you a little report from our annual Babatist convention. I'm so proud to be a Babatist today I could just bust.

We have finally got this denomination on the right track. And it's a wonderful thing to see the precious foot of Jesus mashin' down on the necks of sorry sinners.

As you know, I wasn't so happy last year. Our mighty denomination veered off the road and got into such silliness as apologizing for past racial sins.

Apologizing! Wallowing around like a bunch of sob sisters. Makin' us look plum silly!

We got nothing to apologize for. God made us the largest Protestant denomination in the world! Or, to put it another way, we're the largest religious group in the world actually going to heaven!

Well, this year we didn't get sidetracked by none of that meek-and-mild nonsense. No sir-ree, we was a bunch of bird dogs on point, flushing out coveys of sinners left and right.

Take that Disney bunch. Oh, they had us fooled for a long time with their little mouse ears and cartoons. But if you get to analyzing things, you can see that they were up to no good right from the start.

How come Donald Duck never wore no pants? Think about that. Had all those little "nephews" running around and him naked as a jaybird from the waist down!

And what about that Annette Funnicello and her tight little Mouseketeer sweater? Weren't no boys looking at them big mouse ears, I can tell you that.

And don't even get me started on Snow White. Shacked up with a bunch of midgets! I hate to think what kinds of kinkiness went on there.

Hi-ho, indeed!

Now Disney has really gone off the deep end. Welcoming homosexshuls into their parks just like they was normal!

Well, you won't find any more good Babatists goin' to their little fairyland.

And then there's that other group we got singled out for salvation. Them Jews.

I'll tell you, there's nothing that makes my blood boil quicker than to hear some smart-aleck say, "But Jesus was a Jew."

My eye!

Well sure, he may have been born into a Jewish family on his mama's side. But we can read plain as day in our Bibles that before Jesus started preachin', he stopped by to see his cousin John and get his credentials in order.

And that's cousin John the What? John the Babatist , of course.
John dunked him good. So Jesus may have gone under that water as a half-breed Jew boy, but we all know that he came up as a bona fide Southern Babatist.

Weren't no Lutheran. Weren't no Roamin' Catholic or Bicycling Mormon. Weren't no New Age Hippie-Dippie Crystal-Wearing Nut, neither.

Oh, dear brothers and sisters, we almost let the forces of evil overtake our precious Babatist Convention. And you know who I'm talking about: The "deep thinker" crowd. The "love-one-another" crowd. The "put-that-Scripture-in-context" crowd.

Some people call them "moderates." But I say we go ahead and call 'em by their real name—Methodists!

That's right. They're not Babatists a'tall. They're a bunch of misguided souls on that slippery slope of introspection and contemplation. Oh, dear friends, it's a path that ultimately leads down into the very depths of Presbyterianism.

It just breaks my heart to think about all those lost-as-a-goose sinners out there, wandering around in synagogues and Disney stores. Keep 'em in your prayers, dear brethren and sisterns .

OK, beloved Babatists, enough about that. It's sermon time. Let's all open our Bibles and close our minds . . .

June 19, 1996

A little honest testimony can go a long way

GOSH, I SURE hope I'm not too late with this. I really want to do my part to help.

My old TV preacher friend W.V. Grant and his sweet third wife, Sister Brenda, are set for sentencing in federal court Monday morning. A little matter of tax fraud.

Well, I just found out that I was supposed to be sending the judge a testimonial on their behalf.

But somehow I didn't get the letter—the one their lawyer sent around to all their friends asking them to send Judge Joe Kendall some good words about the Grants' character and reputation and all.

Now that I think about it, I'm wondering if my name got dropped off Brother Grant's mailing list somehow. A computer glitch or something.

Because this isn't the first time I missed mail from them. I didn't get an invitation to Brother Grant's super-duper surprise birthday party at The Mansion on Turtle Creek last year, either.

But anyway, I'm getting off track here. I finally found a copy of lawyer Dennis Brewer's letter asking for testimonials. He says here we should "cite any specific examples of Rev. and Mrs. Grant's life and good deeds that you have knowledge of. Each of you will have special thoughts that you will want to express in the letter to Judge Kendall."

Yes, I certainly have some special thoughts. I think Brother Grant and Sister Grant III are just the bravest little couple I ever knew. Take that surprise party at The Mansion, for example.

I happen to know that the Grants had been going through some awful financial times. Month after month, they sent out letters to their faithful followers just practically begging for money.

And yet that Sister Grant, bless her heart, put up such a brave front by inviting people from all over the country to stay at The Mansion and attend a big dinner party there.

No Motel 6 for their friends. No sir! No backyard birthday weenie roast for the Grants. No way!

Brave, brave, brave.

And this came right on the heels of that terrible tornado that struck their parsonage in DeSoto. Poor W.V. was forced to send out a

"Disaster-Gram" asking supporters to dig deep into their pocket-books and help him out of this tragedy.

Of course, there was kind of a mystery about that tornado. Even though Brother Grant was sending letters across the country asking for money, city officials in DeSoto didn't know of any damage to his home or any house on his street.

A miracle maybe! Hallelujah!

If you ever saw W.V. and Sister Brenda's little parsonage, you know they're truly blessed. It's a $1.2 million estate overlooking Thorntree Country Club. That thing's got nine bathrooms! But I'm sure Brother Grant must need them all.

Well, darn, I'm off the subject again. I'm supposed to be talking about Brother Grant's character. Maybe the best way to do that is to tell about his concern for orphans in Haiti.

See, a while back, things got so bad that Brother and Sister Grant were actually urging their poorest followers to borrow money and send it to them. "I am asking you to borrow $50.00 from a loved one or friend . . . to help me keep this ministry going," Brother Grant wrote, right alongside pictures of pitiful kids in Haiti.

Well, good people kept the ministry going. And Brother Grant got to keep the two Ferraris that were registered in his name at the time. And Sister Grant got to keep going around town in that little Mercedes coupe with the license plate "WVNME."

Aren't they just the cutest couple?

You know, it takes special people to live in a $1.2 million house, drive luxury cars and still humble themselves to beg for borrowed money. But clearly, Brother and Sister Grant are special people.

Mr. Brewer seems to think we can sway the judge with our letters of support. "In one case I observed a federal judge change his mind during the sentencing," Mr. Brewer wrote.

Well, I sure hope this little testimony helps.

July 21, 1996

Successes often sown
by seeds of our failures

A WHILE BACK, my wife and I went to dinner with some teacher friends. One of them, Judy Porter, is a longtime high school teacher in Dallas.

As we ate, one of Judy's former students came in. Judy waved to her across the restaurant. And then she told us a little story.

"When that girl was a senior, she was captain of the drill team. And in the middle of that year, she found out she was pregnant," Judy said.

"Well, after a lot of tears, she called her boyfriend and asked him to come over so she could give him the news. The boyfriend was a year older and already out of school.

"When she told him that she was pregnant, he didn't say a single word. He just got up, walked out of the house, got in his car and drove away.

"The poor girl was devastated. They had gone together a good while, and she thought she knew him. She couldn't believe that he would just walk out like that.

"A couple of hours later, she heard his car pull back in the driveway. The boy came in. He was carrying an engagement ring and an apartment lease.

"And they have been married ever since," Judy said. "It wasn't easy. They have both worked and gone to school. But they stuck it out."

In fact, the whole family was there in the restaurant that night. The young man and woman—and now two children.

No story had filled me with admiration like that one in a long, long time.

You know, we're sort of obsessed with failure these days.

And I understand why that is. We're in the midst of one of those pendulum swings in society. After the permissive, anything-goes mentality of the '60s, we're now swinging back to a mind-set that focuses on right and wrong.

And I suppose it's hard to talk about right and wrong without pointing out when others fail.

With criminals, we talk about "three strikes and you're out." But truthfully, it takes only one strike for us to write people off these days.

The phenomenon is easiest to see in Washington, where politicians and the media are caught up in a game of "gotcha." No failure is ever forgotten.

When Judy told us that story about her former student, she could have focused on the failure—another teen pregnancy, tsk, tsk. But she told the story with pride, focusing not on the failure but on the success that followed. (And by the way, Judy later got the young woman's permission for me to retell the story here.)

This obsession with failure isn't limited to politics and the media. Sometimes, it creeps into the pulpit, too.

Some folks want to use the Bible to divide people—as friends or foes, saints or sinners.

I used to hate reading the Bible because it reminded me that I could never measure up as a saint.

And then one day it suddenly dawned on me: Hey, wait a minute. This book contains the biggest bunch of flops and failures you ever saw.

Old stuttering Moses kept trying to weasel out of being a leader. Mighty King David couldn't keep his tunic on. And those disciples at Jesus' feet were always squabbling—when they weren't missing the point completely.

And when my faith wavers, I think of Peter.

Jesus made that little pun and called Peter "the rock" on which he would build his church. (The Greek name Peter literally means "rock.")

And yet in one night—the night before Jesus' crucifixion—old rock-solid Peter denied even knowing Jesus. Not once, not twice, but three times. Man, what a failure.

Of course, the story doesn't end there.

Today is Easter. It's a day Christians celebrate because it says no failure has to be forever, that fresh starts are always available.

We can go on playing "gotcha," focusing on the failures in others. And in ourselves.

Or we can recognize that failures mean almost nothing. It's what happens next that matters most.

Sometimes those very failures plant the seeds for our greatest triumphs.

A cute little family sitting in a restaurant booth reminded me of that.

March 30, 1997

Some offerings for
Southern Baptist leaders

MEMO TO: Southern Baptist Leadership.

From: A Proud Baptist.

Subject: A Modest Proposal.

First, let me offer my congratulations on another fine convention. Once again, the whole country is talking about the wisdom of Southern Baptists.

Directing women to be submissive was brilliant—and long overdue.

To be honest, I didn't think you could ever match the masterful Disney boycott of two years back. But, by golly, you came close by proclaiming the inferior status of women.

As a follow-up on that issue, we ought to stress that women are responsible for all sin in the world (I Timothy 2:12). And they really need to keep quiet in church, saving questions for their husbands at home (I Corinthians 14:34).

Thanks to your leadership, we Baptists are on quite a roll. And that brings me to my reason for writing.

Before you know it, next year's convention will be here. We should be ready with another great Bible-based truth to proclaim.

We must not nap and allow the "modern interpretation" folks to put their dangerous spin on our scriptures.

So, here's my modest proposal for next year's convention: child sacrifice.

I hope it's not too prideful on my part to imagine the big smile spreading across your faces right now. You're thinking: Of course!

Now that we have put homosexuals and women in their place, it is only natural that we turn our attention to children.

As everyone knows, children are out of control these days. But how different things would be if they understood their precious Biblical role as burnt offerings.

Of course, we all know the famous story in Genesis 22 of how Abraham stood ready to sacrifice Isaac, just as God had instructed. But I'm afraid we have dwelled too much on the happy ending—the last-minute reprieve, the ram in the thicket and all that.

When we read this story to children, we need to focus on how Abraham stacked up a good pile of firewood, how he tied up his boy and placed him on top of the waiting bonfire, how he pulled out his knife and prepared to plunge it into his son . . .

Oh, what a vivid picture for our children to contemplate!

Just imagine how obedient children will become when parents occasionally cock their ears toward heaven, listening for God's instruction to turn them into holy toast.

One little "What was that, God?" ought to get those bedrooms picked up and the trash taken out in a hurry!

Let me suggest that we focus in Sunday school on another Bible story that doesn't get discussed much—the story of Jephthah in the 11th chapter of Judges.

As this leader of Israel prepared to go into battle, he made a vow to God: "If you give the Ammonites into my hands, whatever comes out of the door of my house to meet me when I return in triumph from the Ammonites will be the Lord's, and I will sacrifice it as a burnt offering."

Of course Jephthah whipped those Ammonites like nobody's business. And we read: "When Jephthah returned to his home in Mizpah, who should come out to meet him but his daughter, dancing to the sound of tambourines!"

She was so happy to see her daddy!

But of course, Jephthah wasn't happy to see his only child. "When he saw her, he tore his clothes and cried, 'Oh! My daughter! You have made me miserable and wretched, because I have made a vow to the Lord that I cannot break.' "

Well, children were better in those days, and the daughter said she understood completely. "But grant me this one request," she said to her father. "Give me two months to roam the hills and weep with my friends, because I will never marry."

And the Bible tells us, "After the two months, she returned to her father, and he did to her as he had vowed."

Sad, isn't it? But there it is, straight from the Holy Bible, so I see no room for anyone to disagree.

Well, once again, bless you in your efforts to reduce our Bible to a plain and simple rule book.

It's so much easier than having to read and pray and think.

June 26, 1998

People
Stories

IN THE newspaper business, every story needs a peg. Some might call it an "angle" or a "hook." It's the reason for writing the story.

How lucky I am to be a columnist. I don't need a peg. I only need a person. And "people stories" are among my favorite columns. There's no agenda, no product to plug or ax to grind. The people columns are simply a chance to visit, to get to know someone and hear their stories.

I hope you enjoy getting to know these people. They are some of my favorites. There's quite a range here. Meet Stanley Green, The Funny Man. And Jim Littleton, The Former Man.

Pull up a chair and visit a spell.

Little lessons make lifetime of difference

OVER IN EAST Texas, in my hometown, Teresa Sturrock was honored as "teacher of the year" in the Tyler Independent School District.

She spoke to a civic club there recently and told the story of one student whose life was changed by caring teachers and volunteers.

"Sometimes people wonder if what they do really makes a difference," Mrs. Sturrock told the group. "I'm going to tell you a story about a little boy that shows that the efforts people make really do make a difference.

"This little boy did not have what you would call the most advantageous background," Mrs. Sturrock said. In fact, the boy came from a desperately poor family.

"Neither of the parents had an education above the eighth grade, so it was very hard for them to find jobs," Mrs. Sturrock said.

There were four children in the family. The little boy was third.

"The family of six lived in a tiny one-bedroom duplex. The mother and father and two youngest children slept on beds that filled the small bedroom. The two older boys slept on the floor in the living room.

"Luckily, people in area churches would reach out to the family and take them groceries. Often people would take the children out to buy them clothing," she said.

One time, as winter was coming on, a woman took the little boy out and bought him a green wool coat. "I don't know about your children," Mrs. Sturrock told the group, "but my children have three or four coats and usually don't know where any of them are. But this little boy was so proud of that green coat that he always knew exactly where it was."

At school, teachers went out of their way to make the boy feel smart and capable.

"When he was in the second grade, a teacher appointed him to the grounds committee. Now, that was just a fancy name for the cleanup crew, but the teacher told him, "Any job worth doing is worth doing well." And he worked hard at that job every week.

"Even though he was just on the grounds committee, this teacher was doing great things to instill responsibility in this little boy.

"In the sixth grade, there was going to be a school play and a teacher encouraged the boy to try out for the lead role. And he got it," she said.

Although the parents didn't have much education themselves, Mrs. Sturrock said, they understood the importance of school for their children.

"The night of the school play, the boy's parents were right there on the front row, cheering him on," she said. "That's so important because all children need cheerleaders."

All along the way, concerned people were there to encourage the boy. At one point, he was urged to audition for a part in a citywide musical production, and he got the part.

"When it was over, some of the men got together and presented the little boy with a check for $25 for winning the "Best Actor Award."

"Whether there really was such an award or not, they saw the need and provided for this family. And it was much needed," Mrs. Sturrock said.

Ultimately, that little boy graduated from high school with high honors and went on to college, just as his parents had always said he would—and just as the other three children in the family did.

He earned a master's degree, in fact, and returned to work in the place that had encouraged and nurtured him—the classroom.

"On the first day of his first year to teach, he looked out in the classroom and he saw many faces that looked like his so many years before. He made a vow to give back to the community and to those children some of what had been done for him."

Everything in her story about that little boy was true, Mrs. Sturrock told the group, except for one fact.

"Maybe you have figured out by now,' she said, "that the 'he' in my story is really a 'she.' And she is me.

"In fact, I would not be talking to you as teacher of the year if not for parents and teachers and people in the community who all reached out and helped me."

People might wonder if they can really make a difference. Teresa Sturrock is the answer.

February 20, 1991

House call proves
to be quite a trip

I GET LOTS of column suggestions. But no one had ever sent cash before.

Last week, however, a letter arrived: "I would like Steve *Blow* 's address . . . ," it said in a shaky scrawl. "I'm Ed Connally, 81 years, 2 months, 5 days, and I'd pay him to come to see me if possible."

The letter was signed "Ol' Ed" and contained a worn $5 bill.

How could I resist a visit with Ol Ed? And if nothing else, I needed to deliver his change. I charge only $3 for house calls.

Mr. Connally lives with his daughter and son-in-law in southwest Dallas. He met me at the front door with books in his arms.

"Come on, let's talk out here," he said, leading the way back down the sidewalk with a stooped shuffle. "I've got something I want to show you."

I dutifully followed, wondering where he was headed. My car, that's where.

"Uh, where are we going?" I asked, as he struggled to open the passenger door. "Nowhere," he snapped. "We're going to sit in here."

And so we did. We sat in the front seats and talked for almost an hour. Actually, Mr. Connally talked and I just held on tight for a dizzying ride across the decades, miles of West Texas and every topic under the sun.

"Do you know what religion is?" Mr. Connally asked, not waiting for an answer. "Religion is anything in your mind that leads you somewhere."

And then he offered me the books--one called *The Lost Books of The Bible* and *The Forgotten Books of Eden* , and another, *Catholicism and Christianity* .

I tried to politely refuse, saying I would find copies for myself. Mr. Connally grew adamant. "I'm 81 years old, and they are as worthless to me as teats on a boar shoat!"

I took the books. And looked up "boar shoat." It's a young male hog.

Mercifully, Mr. Connally quickly moved off the religion topic. "In my heyday, I was a rabbit catcher," he said, starting down a rabbit trail that he would often return to. "I roped jack rabbits. I was the No. 1 jack rabbit roper in West Texas."

Most of us are stuck so tightly in the here and now that we have little patience for the mental wanderings of the elderly. On this occasion, I decided to sit back and enjoy the trip. Nevermind that Mr. Connally's conversation wasn't linear, or even logical most of the time. It was like jazz.

"You see, back then, you didn't have all these fandangos," he was saying. "When I was 12 or 13 years old, I got a jackass. You know what a jackass is?"

I said that I did, but Mr. Connally didn't believe it.

"You think you do—until you live with one," he said with the weary air of one who has lived with jackasses.

Mr. Connally was raised around Hico, out west of Waco. "I was born on July 31, 19 and 12, between 11:20 and 12:40 on a Wednesday," he said.

He knows the time because two trains passed the family's house at those times each day. "Mama said when the first train passed, I wasn't there. When the second one passed, I was."

Then suddenly he was back to the rabbits: "I once caught a rabbit—the world's best. And I know he was."

Mr. Connally talked of his many jobs—hauling gravel, his "gift" for pouring concrete, repairing tractor tires torn on plow points. "I went to Mexico once to herd sheep with some guys. I didn't want to go, but I did," he said.

"A fellow there asked me, 'Can you ride a horse?' I said, 'A little.' He said, 'Get on that pony over there and drive those sheep out of the corral.' I said, 'Which direction?' He said: 'Damn the direction. Give 'em hell!' "

Eventually, Mr. Connally seemed to wind down. He paused. "I didn't mean to keep you so long," he said, beginning to climb out of the car. "Well, God bless you. I may never see you again . . ."

I hurried around to help him out, and we walked back to the house. "I caught jack rabbits one night," he said. "It was the best show in the world. I caught 47 one night and another 47 the next night. Never missed a shot."

Mr. Connally stepped inside the front door and I extended my hand in farewell. "So long, Mr. Connally," I said.

"Ol' Ed," he corrected.

So long, Ol' Ed.

October 15, 1993

Sex change ends
storm of inner conflict

MANY OF YOU will remember Jim Littleton, the weekend weatherman for WFAA-TV (Channel 8) during most of the 1980s.

When Jim left the station in 1987, you might say big changes were in the forecast.

Last week, I sat and visited with Jan, the emergency room nurse who once was a TV weatherman, the woman who used to be Jim.

"I did this," Jan explained, "because I wanted to get to a peaceful place in my life. Obviously, this is something I felt very strongly compelled to do."

Jan, who did not want her last name used, now lives on the West Coast. She was back in Dallas for a few days to visit friends.

She said she agreed to talk publicly for the first time about her sex change in hopes of fostering a little more understanding for transgender folks and everyone else who happens to be a little different.

"I'm from the Rodney King school," she said. " 'Can't we all just get along?' "

Not surprisingly, Jan looks a lot like Jim. Or like a sister, anyway. There is that same round, baby face we saw so often on TV. But now the familiar face is set in a new package.

Jan, 41, wore a blue cotton sweater, faded jeans and black cowboy boots. Her hair is sandy blond, wavy and collar length.

I hate to stereotype, but Jan looks like what she is—an ER nurse. She combines a warm, caring face with a slightly tough, no-nonsense manner.

Just like Jim, Jan struggles a bit with her weight. And like Jim, she wears a hairpiece—but wears it much better. It pains Jan to think of the grief poor Jim took over his awkward hairpiece.

And, yes, she has had the surgery that makes her fully a woman. Or at least in no way a man.

But to Jan, the transformation didn't come with the slice of a knife. It happened on the day she moved from Dallas, on Memorial Day weekend in 1988. "I loaded up a U-Haul truck in Dallas as one person and I unloaded that truck in another city as another person. And I never looked back," she said.

Jan doesn't want to say where she moved. But it was there that she underwent the sex-change process—and where she enrolled in nursing school.

"I would have loved to continue doing television," she said, "but I couldn't send out audition tapes because I didn't have any."

He "He—Jim Littleton"—grew up in a very small West Texas town. Even in elementary school, he was thinking about being a girl. And those thoughts just never went away.

"When I was a senior in high school, I wrote my big English research paper on transsexualism," Jan said. "My folks wrote it off to being rebellious."

At Texas Tech, Jim majored in broadcasting and then worked at several West Texas radio stations. That led to a job with a Lubbock TV station, where Jim covered the farm beat and then began doing the weather.

In 1981, Channel 8 offered him its weekend weathercasting job, which Jim would hold for almost seven years.

Throughout that time, Jim was struggling with his sexuality. "I was in therapy the whole time," Jan said. Jim fell in love and married a woman while in Dallas—confessing from the start his internal conflicts.

In 1988, after Channel 8 let Jim go and a brief return to Lubbock TV proved unhappy, Jim decided the time had come to act on his desires. Today, Jan's only regret is the pain her decision caused her parents and former wife. But after an initial rocky period, they have all come to accept her, Jan said.

As a man, Jim was sexually attracted to women, and that didn't change. "I've never been with men and don't have any interest in them," Jan said. "I'm fairly out and active in the lesbian community."

But she isn't "out" as a transsexual except to her most intimate friends. She hates all the sensational stereotypes that go along with transsexualism. "I'm not any of those things. I'm just me and want to be judged as me."

In fact, as we talked, Jan was almost apologetic about the ordinariness of her life. "This ain't the Geraldo show," she said.

"This is just something I did. Some people go in the Army. I went into a gender reassignment program."

January 9, 1994

It's simple: His business is growing

THE ROUGH little shed is almost hidden, tucked back from the road in a shady creek bottom.

A small, hand-lettered sign out front is the only clue that this is a place of business. "Open," it says. "Self-Serve."

Philip White was just sitting down to a plate of leftover roast and potatoes and okra when I stopped by his produce stand in northeast Tarrant County last week.

He wore khakis and a long-sleeved blue cotton shirt. A battered, sweat-stained straw hat hung on a nail nearby.

"Have you had lunch? I'd be glad to share this with you," he offered. I declined to take his lunch but accepted a slice of cake and a soft drink.

Then he began to apologize for the appearance of the place. "Well, I thought I'd have things in better order."

No apologies were necessary. Roadside produce stands are one of my favorite parts of summer. And Mr. White's may be the purest example of the art form in these parts.

For starters, 82-year-old Mr. White grows every single thing he sells.

"I made a good crop of potatoes and onions, but they're about gone now," he said. "I've got peas a comin' in, and I'll have tomatoes and okry awhile longer."

In their seasons, he also sells watermelons and cucumbers and cantaloupes and squash and peppers and eggplant. All that from three acres of sandy loam just a half mile up Big Bear Creek.

And then there's this about Mr. White's produce stand: It's on the honor system.

Most times he's out tending to his vegetable patch, not minding the store. So customers just help themselves. Watermelons are stacked out front. Some produce is in an old kitchen refrigerator. Prices are marked, and there's a little scale for the things sold by weight.

Customers figure their bill and drop the money in a slot next to the tomatoes. "I've got regular customers I never even met," Mr. White said.

Yet all his customers seem to feel a special fondness for Mr. White. Some come bearing gifts. That morning a note was waiting for him when he got to the stand: "Mr. White—There's soup and ice cream in the freezer—Tracil."

"How do you say that name?" Mr. White asked me. I gave it a guess, and he said, "She's a little Mexican girl. I told her one time, 'I can't pronounce that. I'm just going to call you Dolores.' "

Apparently Dolores didn't mind.

Mr. White's wife, Armarilla, passed away four years ago. But he still lives in the stone house up the hill where they raised seven children.

"I was born right up the road here about a mile," he said, motioning northward. "And my dad was, too. He was born in 1876. This property has been in my family ever since it's been owned by anybody."

He grew up farming alongside his father. But like a lot of farm boys, he took a city job in '38, going to work as a machinist for General Dynamics in Fort Worth.

But after 30 years, he'd had enough. "I wanted to get out and see the sky and clouds and rain and such," he said.

He returned to farming the family land, carrying vegetables to the Dallas Farmers Market. "We'd pick one day, and I'd go to town the next," he said.

About seven years ago, that drive got to be too much. And so he scaled back, cobbled the little roadside stand together and began selling his produce there.

His workday still starts "just as soon as I can see," he said. "Now it's not till about 6:30. Earlier in the summer, I could get out there at 6."

The city is now crowding in close on Mr. White's little piece of farm life. The road outside his stand was once just a twisting dirt lane connecting the old communities of Shady Grove and Jellico.

Now it's Davis Boulevard and is being expanded to five lanes, stitching together the bustling corners of Southlake, Colleyville, Keller and North Richland Hills.

In spite of the changes around him, Mr. White is the picture of contentment. "You know, I'm happy at what I'm doing," he said. "I like to work. And I get a little money out of it.

"I can't see just sittin'. Can you? I believe we're put here to do something."

I left Mr. White's produce stand with a watermelon, a cantaloupe and a sack of tomatoes. I figured the bill at $4.

August 2, 1995

Memories thrive
amid lost dreams

IN THE commercial district along Lawnview Avenue in East Dallas, most people know him as simply "the guy who lives in the woods."

Some have taken the time to learn his name—Wyndle Davis.

The few who spend time talking with him are surprised to hear that he once played football for the University of Texas at Austin.

I caught up with Mr. Davis Monday morning. Like most days, he had emerged from the underbrush along White Rock Creek to bum a cup of coffee at Cobb Tree Service. Then he ambled next door for a little conversation at J&J Roofing and Sheet Metal Inc.

I introduced myself and said that I had heard he had been a football star. "Aw, more or less," he said with a shrug.

At age 59, he's still a big bear of a man. He had a bushy beard, a Tyler Pipe gimme cap and a set of clothes badly in need of washing.

Mr. Davis said he grew up in Mesquite. When he was 14, his mother and her seven kids moved to the Buckner Baptist Children's Home.

"Dad got sick. He had a nervous breakdown and was in Terrell," he said, referring to the state mental hospital there. He said he played football for the orphanage's football team, then won a scholarship to the University of Texas, playing there in the late 1950s.

In a matter-of-fact way, he told me his life story—nine years in the Air Force, marriage, a son, divorce. He said he was working at Texas Instruments in the mid-'70s when he got laid off.

"Back then, jobs were hard to come by," he said. "And you can only go so long. It takes money to go out there and chase down jobs."

So at some point he quit trying. And soon was living on the streets.

Off and on for the last 17 years, he said, he has been living in a little camp near White Rock Creek.

Mr. Davis then led me through a lot covered in dumped roofing materials and along a narrow trail surrounded by head-high weeds.

Mr. Davis threw back the blankets draped over one end. "I just turned it into kind of a little motel room," he said. "It keeps me dry and warm."

It wasn't quite like any motel room I had seen. A bare, dirty mattress was on one side. A fetid heap of clothing and foodstuffs filled the other half.

"I have a little grill down by the creek," he said. "I have pots and pans and dishes down there, too."

Mr. Davis seemed to find his living arrangement just fine. "Oh, yeah," he said. "If I didn't, I'd change it."

He said he gets by on $119 in food stamps each month and whatever money he can make picking up aluminum cans.

As we walked back from his camp, I said, "Forgive me for asking . . . ," and then gently inquired if alcohol plays a role in his situation.

"It does," he replied without hesitation.

Back at the roofing company, Mr. Davis settled into a chair by the rear door. He fired up a Basic menthol cigarette, and we talked football a little more.

He said he had played defensive end and wide receiver. The quarterback back then was Joe Cotton. I asked if the team had been good. "Oh, yeah," he said. "We won the national championship two years running. Beat the mess out of Oklahoma."

Clearly, Mr. Davis enjoyed recalling his football glories. "I lived for those days," he said.

When I got back to the office, I called the University of Texas' sports information office to see what more I could learn about Mr. Davis' athletic career.

They had never heard of him. Or a quarterback named Joe Cotton. Or national championships in the 1950s.

"We have this all the time," spokeswoman Sharon Rhodes said. "People claim to have played here. And nine times out of 10, there's no record."

Personally, I think I'll just choose to believe that it's an oversight in the records.

Wyndle Davis may not have much else, but he's entitled to his memories.

October 25, 1995

Requiem for a kindly old farm boy

MR. BARNES died last week. And home just doesn't feel the same right now.

My wife and I were thrilled six years ago when we found a little piece of land out on the eastern edge of town. Lori had always joked that she would be glad to live in the country—"if it could be 10 minutes from a mall." And darned if we didn't find such a spot.

We loved everything about the place—the little pond along the road, the hilltop site for a house, the view at night. But it didn't take us long to decide that one of the best things was the sweet old man who came with the property.

Everett Barnes had been fishing in that pond for 50-some-odd years. And it became clear pretty quickly that a mere change of ownership wasn't going to change that one bit.

And of course that was fine with us. In fact, we found ourselves apologizing repeatedly when all the commotion of building a house interrupted his fishing.

But Mr. Barnes just changed interests for a while and became the unofficial foreman of the project.

Our house is not all that big by modern standards, but to Mr. Barnes it looked like the Taj Mahal going up. As we stopped by the construction site each day, he would greet us with a grin of amazement at the day's developments.

"How many bathrooms y'all gonna put in that house?" he asked at one point. And laughed in disbelief at the answer. Three and a half was two and a half too many to Mr. Barnes.

It nearly pushed him over the edge to one day discover a shower and a bathtub going in side by side in the master bath. Our foolishness was a constant source of amusement to him.

Mr. Barnes was a poor farm boy from Oklahoma. He and his wife lived across the road in a tin-roofed house that would politely be called modest. An indoor toilet was a modern convenience he never had.

Though he didn't have much, he was always generous. He really loved our kids. At Christmastime, he'd come over with a card for each and a dollar inside.

When he found out I was especially partial to the bread-and-butter pickles he and Mrs. Barnes put up every year, he made sure our pantry was well supplied.

After the lottery began, Mr. Barnes was shocked to discover that we never played. To him, it was like free money.

Late one Wednesday night, there was a tap at the back door. It was Mr. Barnes. He had bought a lottery ticket for each of us, and we sat together and watched the numbers pop up.

Mr. Barnes was surprised every time that he didn't win.

He was a masterful porch sitter. He sat out on his front porch in a green metal lawn chair by the hour. And our hectic lifestyle seemed even sillier to us as we zoomed in and out of the driveway a jillion times a day, waving at Mr. Barnes each time.

He would give us a wave and a bemused little smile. I could almost hear him thinking, "I wonder if those people ever get where they're going?"

From time to time, Mr. Barnes inspired us to actually live the slower country life we aspired to. I loved it when he stopped by on Saturday mornings and we'd sit on my front porch and visit.

Mr. Barnes was genuine country, and he gave our place authenticity. He would reminisce about the days when our land was Mr. Greene's farm.

Mr. Barnes had slowed in the last year, and his visits grew rare. After weeks of good intentions, my son and I finally stopped at his house on a recent Sunday afternoon.

He was on the front porch.

He marveled at how Corey was growing. I leaned against the porch railing, where his chickens normally roosted, and we talked of this and that.

Mrs. Barnes called Tuesday night and told us he had died that morning. A stroke. He was 82.

With autumn settling in, leaves are falling from the willows around the pond. That gives me a clear view over to Mr. Barnes' house.

I stand at my front windows and look at that little tin-roofed house. The front porch is empty now. And my own home seems diminished by that absence across the way.

November 19, 1995

No, ma'am, he's not the same Sam

SAM FELDMAN has climbed over an obstacle or two in his life. But he never dreamed that his own name might pose a problem.

"I picked up the phone the other night and a guy immediately started in: 'Oh, Sam, I'm so sorry. Are you all right? Is there anything I can do for you?'

"I said, 'Listen, I need all the good wishes I can get, but you've got the wrong Sam.' "

I suppose Sam's problem could be worse. He could actually be that other Sam Feldman—the one facing as much as five years in a federal slammer.

That other Sam Feldman was the business partner of Dallas City Council member Paul Fielding. And as numerous news reports have made clear, Mr. Feldman and Mr. Fielding are in some hot water.

Mr. Fielding faces fraud and extortion charges. He says he is innocent and is awaiting trial. Meanwhile, Mr. Feldman pleaded guilty to mail fraud and is expected to testify against Mr. Fielding.

And while this drama plays out, Not That Sam Feldman worries about seeing his good name go down the drain. "I didn't think too much about it at first, good or bad," he said. "But the more calls I got, the more it began to bother me."

Not That Sam has never met Other Sam, but they've been getting each other's mail and phone calls for years. And in one unfortunate episode, Sam got served with a lawsuit against Other Sam.

"It was a real mess. I had to hire a lawyer to untangle that one," he said.

Sam, 58, has been a stockbroker here since 1962. And a good one, apparently. I visited him in his high-rise apartment along Turtle Creek—a sleek, stunning home brimming with modern art.

He grew up in my neck of the woods, east of Tyler in Overton. He still talks with an accent that sounds like home to me.

When Sam was just a few years old, he learned that he had muscular dystrophy. It left him with a body that is badly deformed. He has been in a wheelchair all his life.

But a winning personality and a lot of grit more than compensated. Sam was president of his high school class ("There were only 28 of us"), and he won a scholarship to SMU.

But after graduation, all the major brokerage firms turned him down flat. "Things were different for the disabled back then," he said. Finally, Sam found one tiny firm that would give him a chance—on straight commission only.

"I knew if I didn't make it on my own that I would end up living back at home with my family," he said. "Now, Steve, did you want to live at home when you were that age?"

I understood completely.

Needless to say, Sam succeeded. "I admire him because I think he is just so gutty," said one of Sam's customers, H.R. "Bum" Bright. "To have the handicap he has and be as cheerful and outgoing and optimistic as he is, I just think he's a man to be admired and respected."

No, Sam never let his disability deter him. For example:

"Our office used to be on Main Street, on the first floor," he said. "Right across the street was an Avis car rental office. We had a big picture window, and they had a big picture window.

"I really wanted to meet this one particular blond-headed girl over there. So one day I called her up and told her I was in the office across the street. She said, 'Stand up so I can see who you are.' I told the best-looking guy in the office to stand up."

The woman apparently liked what she saw and agreed to go on a date. And Sam showed up.

Her reaction? "I think I was upset," said Helga Feldman, now Sam's wife of 28 years. "I said, 'You should have told me!' "

"Yeah, but with my personality and charm, how could she be mad?" Sam interjected.

Sam's disability has finally forced him to slow down a bit. He gave up driving a few years ago and often works from home now.

But he remains as upbeat and confident as ever—almost. "Everything is great," he said. "If I can get this other Sam Feldman off my back."

You've heard of Sam I Am. Well, this is Sam He's Not.

August 30, 1996

At 89, woman is still leading an octave life

I HAD DINNER with a senior citizens' group recently. And as we ate, an elderly woman played the piano.

Ho-hum, I thought.

There were the usual standards—"Tennessee Waltz," "His Eye Is on the Sparrow." But I began to notice she played beautifully—and without a single sheet of music.

"Isn't that cute?" I thought. "She can still remember those old songs by heart."

And then 89-year-old Margaret Johnson launched into "The Phantom of the Opera." And I don't mean some little two-chord version. I'm talking about a sweeping rendition, grand and passionate.

Hmmm, maybe my ageism had been showing.

I mentioned how impressed I was to the woman seated next to me. And she insisted on introducing me to Mrs. Johnson—at that moment! In the middle of Phantom!

She dragged me over and began a big introduction. Well, Mrs. Johnson never missed a note. She looked up at me with a dazzling smile and said, "Nice to meet you. You need a new picture!"

That settled it—I love this woman!

I went to see Mrs. Johnson this week at her home in North Dallas. And my crush on her only grew.

Little Margaret Bassett was picking out tunes on the piano even before she began taking lessons at age 6. By the time she graduated from Oak Cliff High School (now Adamson) in 1924, she was an accomplished musician.

Her father was Wallace Bassett, the beloved pastor of Cliff Temple Baptist Church for 48 years. And her parents sent her to a small Baptist school in Missouri, expecting her to find a good husband.

"Oh, I met a fellow. He sang and was on pitch and everything, but he wasn't really my type," she said.

Wait. On pitch?

"Yeah," Mrs. Johnson laughed. "I'm kind of funny about people being on pitch. I can't stand a singer who is nearly on pitch!"

So she came back to Texas, to Baylor. And there she met Travis Johnson, a tenor from Troup. And he was on pitch.

"But better than that, he had a job," she said. "And some spending money!"

It was a musical courtship. "He was interested in me because I could play the piano. But when he found out I could transpose, well, that did it. Because you know tenors, they want everything up a third."

Those crazy, key-changing tenors.

They graduated from Baylor in the spring of 1928 and married one week later. They took jobs in Dallas. But Mr. Johnson's heart was in music. And in 1932, they moved to New York.

He landed a job with the staff quartet at radio station WOR. Then, the Johnsons struck out on their own, forming a group of backup singers, The Song Spinners.

They sang on many recording sessions for Decca Records and for a variety of stars of the day, including Ella Fitzgerald. "She was a darling."

"I still hear a lot of our songs on the radio now," Mrs. Johnson said. On the very-very oldies station, of course.

Mrs. Johnson also had an impressive career of her own. Bob Hope hired her to play "Honey Child" on his stage and radio shows. "I was the Southern belle character—slow-talking and kind of dim. But I always got the punch line."

She also had a successful career as an advertising model. "I was the housewife type," she said. "I could hold a baby and they would believe it. Or a vacuum cleaner."

And she wrote advertising jingles—including the classic "Winston Tastes Good, Like a Cigarette Should."

"That's bad grammar, you know," she confided. "It should be as a cigarette should."

Meanwhile, Mr. Johnson went on to a lucrative career as one of the featured singers on the old Mitch Miller Show . Remember singing along with Mitch?

The Johnsons returned to Dallas in the late '60s, and Mr. Johnson died in 1970. But at nearly 90, Mrs. Johnson still goes 90 miles an hour. She plays piano somewhere in town four or five days a week.

"People ask me my secret all the time. I say, 'Two Coca-Colas and a candy bar every day.' Or you can switch it—two candy bars and a Coke."

I love this woman. And I'm thinking of getting a new picture.

March 21, 1997

Funny Man shticks
with what works

BEFORE THERE was Chuck E. Cheese. Before there was Ronald McDonald. Before there were inflatable moonwalk houses and mobile petting zoos, there was Stanley Green.

To several generations of Dallas children, he was Mr. Green the Funny Man—the hit of countless birthday parties.

And somehow, always a mystery, too.

"Hey, what did the dog say when he landed on sandpaper?" Mr. Green asked me. And before I could draw a breath, "Ruff, ruff," he replied. Mr. Green is the master of rapid patter and nonsensical non sequitur.

"What did Tennessee?" Huh? "The same thing Arkansas." What? "The same thing Arkan- SAW !" Oh. . . .

"Hey, you're laughing at my jokes and you're not even looking at my face," he rattled on.

I was talking to 71-year-old Mr. Green on the telephone. "You'll call me back? No, don't call my back. My back don't talk." Or at least I was trying to.

With Mr. Green, you don't talk too much. You mostly play straight man. Even after some 50 years, he's still performing at every chance.

Maybe that's because there aren't too many chances to perform these days. Mr. Green the Funny Man slipped from our midst a few months ago when he moved to a nursing home in Boston.

"Hey, where do Volkswagens go when they get old? The old Volks home!"

Or maybe Mr. Green is always performing because it's his way of deflecting questions and curiosity about the person behind the persona.

"How did I become the Funny Man? I looked in the mirror. What happened to you?"

Doctors tell Mr. Green he has Parkinson's disease. "And Mr. Parkinson can have it back," he said.

"My knees don't work so good now. I can't do the cha-cha-cha. The doctor here looked at my nose, and I said, 'Hey, it's my knees, not my nose.' Knees-Nose. Nose-Knees."

That's the kind of material that made Mr. Green such a killer among the kindergarten set. His shtick was always utter silliness.

"Pick a color. Red? You just fell out of bed. Pink? You fell in the sink. Green? You're a big fat jelly bean. Blue? Go poo-poo-pa-doo."

And the kids would howl.

Yet for the parents, there was always an air of mystery. A poignancy. Word was that Mr. Green lived at the YMCA and walked to all his appointments.

In truth, he lived alone in a little apartment—exactly where, he would never say. And he walked only part of the way. He rode the bus the rest.

Mr. Green never learned to drive. For decades, he was a familiar sight on the streets of North Dallas and the Park Cities, walking along in coat and tie with a big satchel full of his funny props.

Often he had three or four parties on a Saturday. But somehow he got to them all.

He's not sure exactly, but it was about 1950 that Mr. Green put a little ad in the newspaper offering his services as a funny man. A family in Highland Park responded. And from there, word-of-mouth referrals kept him busy. Often he worked among the wealthiest and most prominent families in the city.

As the years went by, he began to visit parties for the children of children he had first entertained. "There must be 50 or 75 people like that," he said.

But time caught up with Mr. Green the Funny Man. His props grew worn and frayed. Children's parties moved from back yards to video arcades.

When Mr. Green began to have health problems, he moved to a Dallas nursing home. But because he had no family here, a brother in Boston coaxed him into moving to a facility there.

"Nobody knows me here. I keep a low profile," he said.

But it can be lonely sometimes, and Mr. Green loves to hear from people in Dallas who remember the Funny Man. He's at The Hebrew Rehab Center, 1200 Center St., Boston, Mass. 02131.

"You have a funny name," Mr. Green told me. "I'll think of you every time I blow my nose."

Mr. Green, Mr. Green, what a jelly bean.

February 22, 1998

Family Matters

FOR A LONG TIME I struggled with one of one the most basic questions people ask: "What's your favorite column?" I'd hem and haw and never quite come up with a satisfactory answer.

Finally, I figured it out. You will find my favorite column here. It's the column I wrote about my dad on Father's Day a few years back. It's my favorite because I wrote it when he could read it.

I hope it's clear that family is a precious thing to me. I tend to write more about the silly moments of family life than the tender ones. Silly is easier. But I sure get sentimental when I think how blessed I was to have the upbringing I did. And I feel an awesome responsibility to try and measure up in raising my own children.

I also feel especially blessed to find the wife I did. She's funny and headstrong, caring and sincere. She's beautiful, inside and out. Even if she does come from a "monkey blood" family.

Maybe money really does grow on trees

I'VE BEEN thinking about wealth lately. But who hasn't, right? Except I've been coming at it from a different direction.

This all started a while back. I was stretched out on the bed one night, watching television. I reached for the remote control, but I picked up the wrong one. I got the one for the TV itself, not the cable converter box. I reached again, and this time I got the VCR remote control.

Finally, I was fumbling with all three remote controls and cursing my luck for having to juggle so many.

And then I suddenly remembered something from a long time ago. I guess I was about 10 at the time, and we had gone to visit some relatives.

They had a brand-new console television with—a remote control!

This was when the gadgets first came out. As I recall, the controller was even shaped something like a ray gun. It was the most amazing and wonderful device I'd ever seen. My brother and I were allowed to stand across the room and perform the magic of turning the TV on and off a few times.

For years after that, the real symbol of wealth for me was a remote-control television.

Now I have a bedroom TV with three remote controls, and I'm mad because of it.

It got me thinking. We never feel rich because we never remember our old measures of wealth. Instead, we're always looking ahead at something new that will surely make us feel rich.

But just like old age, our image of rich is always receding before us.

I remember being envious of cousins who lived in a new house. Most of all, I envied that spray hose on their kitchen sink. Weird, I know. But that nifty trigger sprayer was like the symbol of a modern home.

I grew up in one of the little post-World War II frame houses. So did my wife. I asked her what symbolized wealth to her when she was a child. A brick house, she said, or a two-story one.

We've since lived in both. We've never felt rich.

For that matter, I can't remember the last time I paid any attention to that spray hose on our kitchen sink.

I asked some of my friends and colleagues the same question—what symbolized wealth to them as kids?

A color TV, several said. Store-bought clothes, said one. Eating out in a restaurant, said another. And my favorite—white go-go boots, said one disadvantaged daughter of the '60s.

Just by coincidence, about the time I started thinking of all this, my aunt told a story from her childhood at a family gathering.
Aunt Elmer—her name is really Ozelma, but you know about these family nicknames—was raised deep in the country in East Texas.

"It was in the fall of the year," she said. "We lived on a little farm at Baxter, about eight miles out of Athens. Daddy was a tenant farmer."

Aunt Elmer was about 7 then, which would make it 1932.

"We children almost never went to town in those days—maybe once a year. When we did get to go, it was really something.

"This one time we all went into Athens. Daddy parked the wagon there on the square, and I guess he went off to the grocery store. We children weren't allowed to get out of the wagon. There were seven of us in the family.

"While we were sitting there, a man walked up on the square. His wagon was parked next to ours. He had two apples in his hands.

"An apple to us meant someone was rich. At that time, anybody who had fresh fruit was rich. We might get a piece of fruit at Christmas, but that was about it.

"That man took one of those apples, cut it in pieces and fed it to his mules. I was sitting there just amazed. I just kept thinking how rich that man must be to give an apple to a mule."

Aunt Elmer is not a wealthy person. By most standards, she would be described as one of modest means.

But Aunt Elmer remembers her old measures of wealth. She remembers when a piece of fruit was a luxury.

"Whenever I buy fruit at the grocery store, I still think, 'Well, I must be in the upper echelon,' " she said, laughing at herself. "It makes me feel good to buy fruit to this day."

And that may make Aunt Elmer one of the richest people I know.

April 8, 1990

The shame of
odd names always fades

POOR COREY. The shame has been passed to a new generation.

While helping my 10-year-old son put covers on his school books last week, I noticed that he had written only his first name inside the books. I fussed at him a little for not seeing that he was supposed to write his full name. He didn't say anything.

A few minutes later, when I had finished covering the first book, I took a felt-tip marker and carefully wrote in my best block letters: "Corey Blow—5th Grade."

Now he was forced to speak up. "I wanted you to just put 'Corey' on there," he said.

"Oh," I said, and it suddenly became clear to me what was happening here. The next generation of Blows had discovered the burden of a last name that is, shall we say, unusual.

"I hate my name," Corey confessed when I pressed him on the point. "And I'm not going to that stupid family reunion either," he said.

We merry band of Blows are set to convene in a couple of weeks. It's a small but hardy group.

I told Corey I understood his feelings. And I tried to assure him that the reunion would be a lot of fun. One of the highlights of my youth was getting together with the Blow cousins from San Antonio. We would laugh together about the newest ways we had been taunted, whisper the latest obscene phone calls, and think up blistering retorts.

We were our own little support group—Odd Names Anonymous.

Corey seemed unconsoled, and I really couldn't blame him. I remember well all the teasing I got. Adolescence is tough enough under the best of circumstances, but being named Blow is like a permanent "kick me" sign on your backside.

My colleague in columny, Bob St. John, wrote a while back about the hardships of being named St. John.

Well, let me tell you, my heart bled. Believe me, he doesn't know the meaning of hardship. If he wants trouble, let him spend a few days as Bob St. Blow..

My wife is of Italian descent. Her last name was Territo. She got lots of teasing about that name in school—Frito, Dorito, etc. She said her one consolation was knowing that one day she would get married and change her last name to something normal.

Isn't life funny?

The special hardship of the name Blow is that it has some unfortunate slang meanings. I won't dwell on that, but take my word for it, the teasing can get especially rough in junior high, where it's every boy's duty to be as mean and vulgar as possible.

And then there are meanings you don't even know. As a reporter, I covered a sensational trial in which two undercover cops, a man and woman, were accused of using more cocaine than they confiscated.

A few days after they were convicted, I bumped into them in their lawyer's office. "We couldn't believe your name," the guy said to me. It seems that "blow" is a street name for cocaine.

"It was hilarious to see your byline on those stories," he said. "Every morning we read your stories and just started laughing all over again."

I was glad I could be of some comfort to them.

Colleague John Anders enjoyed pointing out in one of his name games columns that my byline was especially apropos when I wrote about (and rode out) Hurricane Alicia from the battered Galvez Hotel in Galveston.

These days I don't get teased too much about my name—not to my face, anyway. That's the difference between kids and adults.

The one exception is in angry letters. When I step on toes, the letter-writers just can't resist. For example:

* "A lot of smelly hot air did BLOW in your article."
* "To hell with Cardinal Blowhard . . . ."
* "Mr. Blow is just a little too breezy for my tastes."
* "The man needs to go blow his horn elsewhere, maybe in Tooterville."
* "Is Blow your real name?"

Yes, it's a real name. And I wish I could spare Corey the next few years of hardship it will bring. I wish I could let him see that the "kick me" aspects do eventually fade.

Somehow, in fact, after all the misery is over, you even begin to feel proud of it.

Kind of like a gallbladder scar, I guess.

September 2, 1990

A good turn can really put you in a fix

I'M WONDERING about the etiquette for those family-photo Christmas cards you receive from casual acquaintances. Is it OK to throw them away with the rest of the Christmas cards?

One morning last week, I left the house in the usual dither—running late, dirty laundry tucked under my arm, briefcase in one hand, a sloshing cup of coffee in the other.

I backed out of the garage and was about to zip away when I noticed a piece of escaped trash in the middle of the driveway.

A second look and I recognized it as one of those photo Christmas cards. Now, I may not know the exact etiquette on this issue, but I do know that it's bad form to have family photos blowing around the neighborhood.

So I zoomed back into the driveway to retrieve the card. I threw open the door of the mini-van, bumped the gear shift lever into neutral and swung around in the seat to step out.

At least I thought I had put it in neutral.

Suddenly, there I was, sitting sidesaddle in a lurching mini-van. Lurching, unfortunately, directly toward the closed garage door.

The lurching didn't last long. It was quickly followed by bashing. And then some smashing.

I thought to myself: Remain calm. Think quickly. Who can you blame this on?

I thought of blaming the kids for spilling trash in the yard. Except they have the perfect alibi—they never take the trash out.

I surveyed the damage. The door was still standing. It just looked like it had taken a drive on North Central Expressway. The van was unhurt.

I called Lori at work and told her not to open the garage door when she got home. "Why?" she asked excitedly.

She later confessed that for one fleeting moment she thought I was going to surprise her with a new car.

See why I love her? In 20 years, I've never surprised her once with an extravagant, spontaneous gift. And yet she keeps hoping.

What a dope.

When the kids got home from school, I called the house. I knew they wouldn't have seen the door yet.

"Don't try to open the garage door," I told my darling, surly 13-year-old daughter. She didn't skip a beat. "What (implied: dumb thing) have you done now?" she asked.

See why I love her?

I spent the next couple of days trying to summon the courage to call a repair company. I just couldn't bring myself to spend a couple of hundred dollars to fix a door that was perfectly good until some idiot ran into it. Even if the idiot was me.

Then, driving home from work one evening, I was suddenly overwhelmed by the feeling that I was a man, by George, and ought to get out there with a big hammer and fix that garage door.

Did you know that a garage door is a very complicated piece of machinery? Neither did I.

I admit that I have always taken garage doors for granted. They go up. They go down.

But as I began disassembling mine, I learned that there are some high-tension springs and cables you just never notice. I noticed them when a cable nearly took my hand off.

And then, once you undo those cables, the door is free to slam itself into the ground like a runaway freight train. Very exciting.

By 10 p.m., most of the garage door was in pieces on the garage floor. The rest of it was hopelessly wedged in the frame. It wouldn't go up. It wouldn't go down.

I could have just given up. But no. I did what any self-respecting, self-reliant, nearly-40-year-old man would do.

I called Daddy.

Some people are blessed with great wealth. Some with good looks. I am blessed with a great dad. Who travels with his own tools.

The next evening, Mom and Dad came over from Tyler for a nice visit and a few hours of reconstructive garage-door surgery.

Amazingly, we got the door put back together. We even got it straightened out and working pretty well.

I'm not sure, I probably still need to replace a couple of panels on the door.

But I'm sure of this: Always save family-photo Christmas cards.

February 7, 1992

Ya'll pass le barbeque, see voo play

WE'VE HAD an international sort of summer at our house. And we never even left Texas.

Foreign culture came to us this year in the form of a 16-year-old exchange student from France.

His name is Frederic Marie Michel Francois Maubert.

We call him Fred.

It's been a wonderful time, and we've all learned a lot.

Fred comes from Le Havre, a port city on the northern coast of France. Before he arrived, we pronounced it Lah HARVE, with the harshest possible Texas accent.

Now we know to mumble LooAHVruh, with the smoothest, silkiest French accent possible.

We can all count to 10 in French now, but we're still practicing on "quatre" (four). You pronounce it like cat with a little hairball at the end.

The primary purpose of Fred's visit, however, was not for us to learn pidgin French but for him to practice his English. And he's done splendidly.

Of course, the notion of sending someone to Texas to learn English is a real hoot. I have this image of Fred as an international business executive someday: "Pierre! Emile! Y'all git me that there bidness ree-port, see voo play."

Over the last seven weeks, Fred has fit right into our family. People even say he looks like us. And he seems to have taken no offense at this.

Corey is the only member of the family who had any real adjustment to make. He gave up his bed and spent the summer sleeping under the ping-pong table.

I've slept fine, thank you.

For those who wonder, no, 13-year-old Allison did not develop a crush on Fred. But two of her best friends are goners.

Shortly after Fred arrived, my wife, Lori, asked him what foods he doesn't like. She wanted to plan meals accordingly.

At first, Fred said he liked everything. At our insistence, however, he confessed that he doesn't like rognon.

Rognon? we asked, scratching our heads.

Finally, Fred resorted to his French-English dictionary. "Ah," he said, "kidneys!"

"No problem," promised Lori.

It has sometimes been daunting to see American culture through a visitor's eyes. I walked into the den one Sunday afternoon and found Fred watching "Gilligan's Island." I wanted to apologize on behalf of all Americans everywhere.

But it's been nice showing off our national achievements. In Europe, Fred said, they don't have drive-up windows.

It's also fun listening to 12-year-old Corey try to explain American culture to Fred—such as a convention of Elvis impersonators. Some things just defy explanation.

Corey has been especially eager to learn French culture. An overheard conversation: "Do you have cuss words in French?"

"Yes."

"Will you teach 'em to me?"

Fred wasn't too impressed with Galveston beaches ("a chemical wasteland"). But from the top of Enchanted Rock near Fredericksburg, he found the Texas of his imagination. "This," he said, looking out over the Hill Country panorama, "is what I pictured Texas to be."

We all sat attentively as Fred tasted his first bite of Mexican food. "Good," he proclaimed. "Strange, but good." And we laughed along with him as he tried to dance the Cotton-eyed Joe.

We tried to impress Fred with our extensive examples of French culture here in Texas. I think he was especially awed by the Cafe de France at the Hillsboro factory outlet center.

To try to make him feel at home, we served him French toast, French rolls and French dressing. But when he didn't recognize any of them, we began to suspect he might be an impostor from Oklahoma.

Though he's been unfailingly polite, Fred has expressed dismay at some of our foods—like our neon yellow mustard ("That's not mustard"), our pasteurized processed cheese food ("That's not cheese"), and our low-cholesterol squeeze-bottle imitation-flavored butter-substitute spread ("That's NOT butter").

Unfortunately, Fred goes home tomorrow. We will certainly be sad to see him go. He's part of our family.

But we will always have something to remember him by—Corey speaks with a French accent now.

August 23, 1992

Decision about
family planning not a real pain

WHEN I TOLD my boss that I needed to take off a little early last Friday, he laughed and said, "Are you going to write about this?"

When my wife blabbed to friends about my plans, they cackled and said, "Are you going to write about this?"

When the doctor entered the little operating room, where I reclined, feet in the air, he promptly asked, "Are you going to write about this?"

Frankly, I'm offended. What kind of person would be so shameless, so tasteless, so utterly lacking in decency as to write about his own vasectomy?

Well . . .

Honest, I didn't plan to write about this. But there sure is a lot of curiosity out there among my brethren concerning this particular procedure. And when the nurse came at me with the adhesive metal plate, I knew what I had to do.

To heck with privacy. Brothers, this is public service.

The fundamental decision to have no more children was easy. Two teen-agers at home will erase those doubts. So that left only the fear factor.

I slinked into Dr. Keith Newman's office at 3 p.m. Friday. Naturally, for the first time in human history, there was no wait in a doctor's waiting room.

"Are you ready to get started?" a cheerful nurse asked immediately. "Yes," I lied.

I had hoped that skipping lunch would be the worst requirement in this little process. But it got ugly quick.

"Go ahead and undress," the nurse said. "But leave your shoes and socks on."

Oh, the indignity! The only thing more shameful than nakedness is nakedness with shoes.

"You will be putting your feet up in stirrups," the nurse explained. "Shoes will make it more comfortable."

Clearly, this was going to be worse than imagined. Maybe babies wouldn't be so bad.

At this point, the nurse unwrapped a large metallic patch with a wire dangling from it.

As she affixed the adhesive plate to my bare right rump, I couldn't help asking about its purpose. She replied, and I will quote her exactly, "It's a ground wire."

A ground wire!? Were we expecting lightning?

She plugged me into a menacing piece of electronic equipment - a "coagulator"—and said, "When he starts using this, you'll want to be grounded."

When he starts using that, I thought, I'll want to be unconscious.

Dr. Newman came in about that time, along with a "colleague." He introduced us, but I don't recall the fellow's name. I'm terrible with names when naked.

Dr. Newman said his colleague would be "assisting" him. But from their hushed conversation, it became clear that this was a teaching situation.

Now, I don't mind getting a trainee at McDonald's. And once I let a student hygienist clean my teeth.

But some things are too important for practice.

I swear, if the guy had said "oops" just once, I was climbing down off that table, shoes and all.

But just as the fear of a Bobbitectomy filled my mind, Dr. Newman was kind enough to administer an intravenous dose of Valium. "A six-pack," he called it in technical medical terminology. And suddenly, all my worries floated away.

A sheet draped across my knees kept me from seeing anything. But the good doctors seemed to work much harder than I expected. I thought it would be just a simple matter of snip, snip.

Instead, it seemed more like an engine overhaul. I swear at one point they were using a ratchet wrench, a hammer and a soldering iron.

The doctor kept asking if I was OK. I assured him that I was quite accustomed to such pain.

In journalism, it's called editing.

No, seriously, guys, it really wasn't bad at all. In just 30 minutes, the work was done. Very smooth, Dr. Newman pronounced. And I wobbled home.

And best of all, under strict doctor's orders, I spent almost the entire weekend stretched out on the couch.

Couldn't mow the lawn. Couldn't wash the car. Couldn't even help with the dishes.

Not a bad weekend—even with an ice pack in your lap.

May 6, 1994

The little gifts add up
to one that's priceless

IN MY 42 Christmases, I have received some wonderful gifts. There was the year my brother and I got a go-cart. Man, that was fun.

My wife splurged one lean year and bought me a set of *Encyclopaedia Britannicas*. I spent Christmas Day browsing from Aalto to Zwingli. Yeah, I know. I'm a nerd.

With a little thought, I can recall lots of other great gifts. Lincoln Logs when I was about 6. A super-duper chemistry set when I was 12. A .22 rifle when I was a teenager.

But it's funny, of all the gifts, the ones that spring to mind first each Christmas season are the little ones that my grandfather brought to us kids each Christmas Eve when he arrived home from work.

Granddaddy worked the evening shift at the post office, sorting mail from noon till mid-evening.

(And here's one measure of the man: One of my distinct childhood memories is of Granddaddy sitting at home practicing his mail sorting. He had a miniature mail case and small cards addressed like letters, and he would sit there flipping those cards into the appropriate slot, striving to improve his efficiency.)

As I think about my grandfather now, I realize what a man of contradictions this Otto Orville Kent was. He was very cautious, if not downright overprotective, about physical danger.

But then Nana and Granddaddy lost a precious daughter, 4-year-old Linda, in a playground accident in 1942. (A swingset toppled over on her.) Now that I'm a parent, I realize how such a thing could change you for life.

Yet, to the delight of his grandchildren, Granddaddy could also be the silliest, most carefree fellow alive.

At our insistence, he would periodically make a little mouse out of his handkerchief and magically make it run up his arm, pretending to be highly alarmed by this runaway rodent.

He often took his guitar down from a nail on the wall to sing us funny songs, like the one about the goat who ate a shirt right off the line. There was a man, now please take note. There was a man, who had a goat . . .

Granddaddy loved riddles and wordplay. Sometimes he would tell us to spell his name backward. "O-t-t-o," we would dutifully reply. "No, that's frontward," he would say. "Spell it backward."

"O-T-T-O!" we would howl.

"That's called a palindrome," Granddaddy would say, then challenge us to think of more. "Tot," "pop," "kook," we would say.

Then Granddaddy would rip forth with one like "A man! A plan! A canal! Panama!"

Though he had only a fifth-grade education, Granddaddy was a man of enormous intelligence. He taught himself Spanish well enough to work as a translator for the government during World War II.

I can remember him reading Cervantes in Spanish. For fun. He loved languages and also dabbled in French and Russian and German.

Whatever appreciation of words I have, it undoubtedly came from Granddaddy, both directly and through Mom and my Uncle Jan.

My grandfather was a gracious and gentle man, but he also held deep convictions and didn't shy from speaking his mind. I'll never forget the Sunday when Granddaddy stood up in the middle of the preacher's sermon and stopped him.

"Just a minute, Brother Kenneth," he said, and proceeded to speak for the congregation on some point of theological error (while I tried to melt into the pew).

As I said, Granddaddy worked evenings at the post office. So the family Christmas Eve get-together would be going strong by the time he got home from work.

But every year, Granddaddy would make his jolly entrance with some sort of little extra gifts for all us kids. This was in addition to whatever regular presents Nana and Granddaddy had bought us.

One year he bought flashlights for all of us. Another year it was inexpensive pocket watches. Often we also got our very own box of chocolate-covered cherries.

Granddaddy took such delight in passing out these gifts. And we received them in the same spirit.

My grandfather died suddenly in 1969, just 12 days before Christmas. I'm sure that's also a big part of why I think about him so much this time of year.

Today I couldn't possibly find any of those little gifts Granddaddy gave us. But the memory is mine forever.

December 25, 1994

Move unearths four decades of life, memories

MY MOTHER-IN-LAW moved last weekend.

That's so easy to say. And so painful to do.

It's not just that we had almost 44 years' worth of stuff to deal with—although that was painful enough.

But we also had 44 years' worth of memories to contend with.

It was January of 1953 when Louis and Maurine Territo took the plunge and paid a whopping $10,500 for a brand new house in Pleasant Grove.

And there they raised a family. And apparently made it a firm policy never to throw anything away.

In a lot of ways, their home mirrored the one where I grew up—a tidy frame house in a neighborhood of kids and station wagons and tight budgets. Just like my house, a den was added in the '60s.

Lori's family mirrored mine as well—a mom, a dad, two big brothers and a princess.

Maybe all those similarities are what made the house comfortable for me from the beginning.

I remember well the first time I visited there. I was a nervous 19-year-old kid from Tyler, carefully following directions through big scary Dallas.

It was the summer of 1971. Lori and I had met a few weeks earlier in Galveston. And she still gives me grief for showing up wearing a purple Ban-Lon shirt.

Remember Ban-Lon?

The really sad part is that I went out and bought that shirt especially for the occasion.

She couldn't have hated it too terribly. We were married six months later.

Lori's dad was this big, gruff-talking Italian character, a papa bear who scared me to death. But I quickly learned that mama bear Maurine was really in charge. And she was a fellow East Texan who made me feel at home from the start.

All those memories came back anew as we prepared for the move, sifting and sorting through closets and storerooms.

It was kind of like an archaeological dig through four decades of Americana.

We unearthed skateboards with steel wheels and plastic-bonnet hair dryers and macrame wall hangings and men's white belts and hair rollers the size of soup cans and whole wardrobes of double-knit.

We actually found clothes so far out of style that they are back in style—at least according to my teenage daughter.

Strange treasures abounded in all this flotsam and jetsam of family life. I now have on my desk a medallion from the 1964 New York World's Fair "Festival of Gas."

We played stump-the-kids as we cleaned out rooms. They were mystified by stretcher contraptions for drying jeans wrinkle-free (theoretically) on a clothesline.

They were completely stumped by a razor strap—and I had a hard time explaining a straight razor to them and how it could be sharpened with leather.

But I must say I now understand why kids behaved so well in olden days. Man, that razor strap hurt when we traded playful swats.

While a home is full of wonderful memories, it holds sorrows, too. And the move stirred those as well.

It was in that home on Traymore Avenue that my in-laws learned that their oldest son had been killed in a car accident just a mile away.

It was in that home that my father-in-law suffered a devastating stroke in 1982. He spent the last seven years of his life in a wheelchair, unable to speak, but still delighting in all the family life that swirled around him.

The passage of time is strange. It seemed like one day that I was quaking at his gruff bark. And it seemed like the next that I was helping bathe him and care for him—feeling a tenderness for the old bear that I could never imagine.

As it turned out, I was the last person to leave the house. I had gone back Monday evening to clean the last few things out of the garage. Rain was peppering down. The empty house echoed strangely. And memories pressed close around.

When the last few items were loaded, I paused a moment to take a final look. And closed the door.

October 27, 1996

The be-all and end-all of cure-alls

I SHOULD HAVE known this marriage was going to be rocky. Lori and I come from very different backgrounds.

I come from a Campho-Phenique family.

Lori comes from monkey-blood people.

(And I would love to see the expressions on the faces of younger readers right now as they wonder what this weirdo is talking about.) What I'm talking about, of course, is the preferred cure-all for life's little bumps and scrapes.

In my house, the little green bottle of Campho-Phenique was like a sacred vial. A magic potion enshrined in the medicine cabinet.

And, of course, there was always a sewing needle tucked into the label. A needle dipped in Campho-Phenique was the perfect surgical instrument for extracting splinters, thorns and small internal organs.

Lori's family, on the other hand, firmly believed that monkey blood was the only reliable cure. I guess Mercurochrome is the proper name, but monkey blood is so much more descriptive.

I was always sort of jealous of kids from monkey-blood families. With monkey blood, you were guaranteed to get sympathy. It was like a big, bright red-orange sign that said, "I have sustained a recent injury, but I'm being very brave about it."

With Campho-Phenique, you just smelled funny.

All of this comes to mind because my daughter woke up the other morning complaining of a little ulcer in her mouth. And I was shocked to hear myself prescribe Campho-Phenique. I hated it when Dad said that when I was a kid.

Campho-Phenique is bad enough on the outside, but putting it in your mouth is really disgusting. But it also works.

More and more these days, I'm astounded to hear my father's voice coming out of my face. "Just dab a little Campho-Phenique on it. It won't hurt you."

Not for internal use? Pish and posh. That's just lawyer talk.

(Lori swears that her monkey-blood family actually swabbed throats with the stuff when they had sore throats.)

I guess it could have been worse. I knew iodine families. And alcohol families. And I heard tell of coal-oil families.

The sad truth is that I always wanted to be a Bactine family.

It's not just that Bactine was guaranteed not to sting. Bactine families were modern families. They were families that ate in front of the television, kept Cokes in the refrigerator and gave their kids folding money for allowance.

I come from a family that firmly believed water is just fine, "four bits" is plenty of allowance and you can't trust a medicine that doesn't hurt.

A few months ago, my teenage daughter took a nasty fall while bike riding in the neighborhood. (And by the way, thank you, thank you again to the sweet readers who stopped and delivered both Allison and her bicycle back to the house.)

Well, poor Ali was a pitiful sight. She had scraped all the hide off her knees and elbows.

I took one look at her and knew what I had to do. I jumped in the car and raced to the nearest store. By gosh, in this moment of crisis, we were going to be a Bactine family!

They didn't have any.

I brought back some other spray stuff that was supposed to be no-sting. It wasn't.

We treated her wounds with much sympathy and furious fanning and blowing to try to take the sting out.

Then, when she got to volleyball practice at school the next day, athletic trainer (and family friend) Sarah Wolfskill called her in for professional treatment.

The ever-gentle "Coach Wolf" proceeded to scour the wounds with Comet and a wire brush. At least, that was Ali's version.

So much for being a Bactine family. But it was amazing how quickly the wounds healed.

In my next medical lecture, I'll cover my family's myriad uses of hot salt water.

Sprained ankle? Soak it in hot salt water. Sore throat? Gargle with hot salt water.

(Preferably not the same water.)

December 1, 1996

New year offers a
holiday gift from the heart

AS WE FINALLY headed out into the Kansas night, my son said, "So, are you going to write about this?"

At 16, he's savvy enough to know that the best column fodder often comes from life's little setbacks. And we'd just had one.

Our otherwise perfect skiing vacation in Colorado ran into a setback of the mechanical sort as we headed home on New Year's Day.

I had noticed an odd little whine when we stopped for gas in Denver. As we drove across Kansas, it turned into a growl. And by the time we limped into a truck stop in Salina, it sounded like we were grinding out scrap-metal sausage.

The alternator was clearly kaput.

We were traveling in a caravan with three other families, so I had plenty of moral support/merciless taunting in this moment of crisis.

I insisted that the others go on. "No way," said head taunter Dickie Dunn. "If we go off and leave you, you'll write about us leaving you stranded."

He smiled and took another sip of his Coke.

There is something worse than being stranded on the highway alone. That's being stranded on the highway with hecklers.

(Dickie happens to be associate pastor of our church. He thinks the Great Commission was to go forth and do comedy.)

The chances of finding a mechanic shortly before 5 p.m. on New Year's Day seemed nil. But I grabbed a battered Yellow Pages, borrowed quarters from everyone in the group and started working the pay phone like a Vegas slots fiend.

I guess I sounded pitiful enough that the answering service for Clare Generator Service put me through to the home of an employee. And he agreed to come!

With help on the way, I persuaded my traveling band of hecklers to head on to Dallas—and to take my weary family with them. It would be midnight before they got home, and way up in the wee hours before I could make it.

That's when my son volunteered to stay with me, and I quickly welcomed Corey's company.

The good Samaritan-repairman not only came, but brought a co-worker with him. "I've got to warn you, you're looking at two parts guys," the partner said, meaning they're not regular mechanics. "But I think we can get you fixed up."

Hey, no problem. When it comes to auto repairs, two parts guys beat one whole journalist every time.

And so, after some three hours' delay, the sausage grinder was surgically removed and a new alternator was quietly alternating under the hood.

Corey and I started for home. And that's when he asked, "So, are you going to write about this?"

"Oh, I doubt it," I said. Then I asked, "If you were writing a column, what would you say about this experience?"

"It could be about appreciating the little things," he said. "Like finding two guys willing to leave their families on New Year's Day to fix your car."

We said nothing more about column writing, but went on to talk about a little of everything else.

Teenagers normally come in three flavors—silent, sulky and surly. But Corey seemed to take seriously his duty to keep me awake. And so we talked.

We pondered the difference in gasoline and diesel fuel. And sang along with oldies on the radio.

He told me that he aced a quiz over state capitals this year because in fifth grade I taught him that Ver-MONT's capital is MONT-pelier.

I didn't even remember that, but I was tickled that he did.

"Are you sleepy?" he asked as we neared Oklahoma City.

"No," I said. "Are you?"

"Yeah," he confessed. "How about if I take a nap now and help you drive later?"

"That's a good plan," I said. And in matter of minutes, he was sound asleep in the seat beside me.

As Corey slept, it occurred to me that I had the answer to his question. Yes, I ought to write about this night. I ought to take note that setbacks sometimes turn into chances to appreciate little things.

Like two fellows willing to help a stranded family on New Year's Day.

Like the chance to share a night with your son.

January 5, 1997

A kid is never lost
if he has a dad like mine

IT WAS ONE of my very first dates, and I was a nervous wreck. Me. A girl. A car. Alone. Yikes.

But somehow it went OK. We had managed to make conversation. I hadn't spilled anything. The evening was almost over. And then disaster struck.

Suddenly, the car just quit. Kaput. And my heart almost did, too.

I coasted into a service station. And I tried and tried to restart the car. I got out, raised the hood and attempted to look knowingly at the engine.

Finally, I did the unthinkable. I called my Daddy.

When Dad arrived, he peered under the hood. He got in and tried to start it. I stood off to the side, making humiliated small talk with my date.

Then Dad called me over to the car, as if we needed to confer man to man about this perplexing mechanical problem. And he whispered, "You ran out of gas."

But . . . but . . . that was impossible! We were at a gas station!

Dad grinned. "I know," he said. "But you don't have to tell her. Just take my car and say I'm going to stay here and try to get this one started."

So I took my date home in the family station wagon—a final act of humiliation. And Dad stayed behind with the only car that ever ran out of gas at a gas station.

The funny thing is that I don't remember for sure who the girl was. But what I remember perfectly is how Dad tried to spare me embarrassment.

I think almost any father in the world would be tempted to have a little fun at his son's expense in that situation. Me included.

But not my dad.

Do you mind if I use this Father's Day to unabashedly brag on my own father?

Trust me when I say no one deserves it more than Alton Blow of Tyler. "Skeet" to his family and friends.

In Sunday school awhile back, the teacher asked everyone to think of the very best person they have ever known. Mother Teresa didn't count, he said. It had to be someone we knew personally.

Others in the class gave their answers and the discussion moved on. But at home that afternoon, my wife asked, "Who were you thinking of in Sunday school?"

"Dad," I said. "Me, too," she said. Of course.

Oh, I'm sure he must have some flaws. But darn if I can think of what they are.

"Genuine"—that's a word that comes to mind when I think of Dad. A "real man," but not in the sense of some he-man or macho guy. Just real. Really firm in his beliefs. Really kind in his outlook. The person I saw at home was always the person I saw in public.

"Selfless"—there's another good word. He has always stood ready to help someone else. Whether it was jumping up from the dinner table to do the dishes—or coming to my house to help me build a fence. Sometimes when I sit in my back yard now, I can't help but admire that white picket fence, so perfectly straight and true. Like a reflection of Dad himself.

It seems so unfair that someone so good should have to get sick. But Dad's dealing with a tongue-twister ailment right now— olivopontocerebellar atrophy. It's something like Parkinson's.

His walk and his talk are pretty wobbly these days. But I know that on the inside, a steadier man never lived.

After my daughter's high school graduation ceremony a few weeks ago, I was reminded of something I hadn't thought of in many years.

A mob was pouring out of Reunion Arena that evening. Our group got separated in the crowd. But up ahead I could easily keep an eye on Dad.

It reminded me that when I was a little kid, I discovered something very reassuring. Dad is tall and thin. After a few of those panicky episodes of finding myself alone in a store or a crowd, I discovered that all I had to do was step back and look above the shelves or above the crowd, and I would see Dad's curly hair.

As we left that graduation ceremony and I kept Dad in sight up ahead, it occurred to me just how lucky I have been.

To have a father who stood above the crowd and made his children feel they would never be lost. . . . What more could I ask?

Alton Blow died March 16, 1998.

June 15, 1997

Slumgullion

MY WIFE'S grandmother, Lucy Cook, was poor as gully dirt. But Granny could whip up a delicious meal out of the least little bit of food. And then, because nothing was ever wasted, she would mix the leftovers into a delicious stew she called "slumgullion." A little of this. A little of that. Never the same twice.

I think of Granny when I write one of those hodgepodge columns—a little of this, a little of that. I thought of her as I pulled this chapter together. It's a real slumgullion-style mixture of columns. You will find a family tragedy, a ghost story, several columns of pure silliness and a favorite story about God moving in mysterious ways.

Foreign terms sound erudite?
Au contraire

IF THERE IS one thing that really chaps my *derriere*, it's people who toss around fancy foreign words and phrases.

Whenever I hear someone talk about a *raison d'etre*, I can't help but think, "What a jerk *extraordinaire*."

Maybe it's a reflection on my state of Texas public education, but I'm usually stumped by anything in italics.

Maybe that's the language I should have studied in school— Italics 101: *Lingua franca* of the *beau monde*.

I took Spanish.

I struggled with *film noir* for a long time. And just about the time I figured it out, along came *cinema verite*.

I think I was the last person to realize that "dining *al fresco*" meant "eating outside."

Hey, why didn't they just say so?

So *nouvelle cuisine al fresco* would be "deer-meat tacos with mosquitoes." In East Texas, we call that *le camping*.

To dramatize this language crisis, let's look at last week's issue of *Time* magazine. First, here's a small item noting that the designer Erte is "remodeling his *finca* on Majorca."

And there's nothing worse than a rinky-dinky *finca.*

A *finca,* by the way, is a Spanish plantation or estate. Try working that into a conversation.

A few pages over in that same issue of *Time* we read of a chef who "brings sadistic elan to his dicing, flaying and serving of *les poissons.*"

And this is in a review of a Disney cartoon, no less. Let's see, les poissons. Something tells me that might be French for fish. Or chicken. Or poison.

Still a few pages further, we find this intriguing question posed in an article on a new building at Ohio State University: "Did the university want a *fin-de-siecle* monument to erudite monomania, inspired nervousness, the intriguing lunatic gesture?"

And I say, Huh?

I'm left wondering: Did the writer want us to stop reading at that particular spot or did he prefer that we not start the article at all?

I asked an erudite colleague what *fin de siecle* might mean. He said he thought it meant the end of something, or literally, the end of a cycle.

Oh, I get it. Like, after the spin cycle comes the *fin de siecle*.

Well, it turns out that it literally means "end of the century." And the definition is "formerly used to refer to progressive ideas and customs, but now generally used to indicate decadence."

Oh.

As we approach the 1990s and another *fin de siecle*, it looks like *fin de siecle* will be the word *du jour*.

Incredibly, that same *Time* also mentions a "video sculpture"—whatever that is—titled *Fin de Siecle* II. And the new issue of *Esquire* refers to "*fin de siecle* Vienna."

Yes, yes, I recognize that many foreign words are lovely and perfectly appropriate. Some are irreplaceable. *Deja vu*, for example. *Deja vu*, for example.

And I know that foreign words enrich and enliven our language. It's not all a matter of snob appeal.

I don't think my kinfolks in East Texas were putting on airs when they would say, "We got *beaucoup*s of okra this year." It's hard to be uppity about okra.

The first time I saw *beaucoup* in print, I didn't have a clue that this was the familiar East Texas word "boo-coo," meaning "a heap of" or "a mess of."

No, I'm not talking about those foreign words. You know the words I mean—the high-falutin ones designed to call attention to themselves.

Awhile back, a snooty secretary said to me on the telephone, after I had asked to speak to her big-shot boss, "And this is *in re* to?"

I wanted to reply with some clever *bon mot*, such as "Shut up, stupid."

But that seemed a breach of business etiquette, so I merely answered her question and thought to myself, "What a pretentious pea-brain."

And so I offer this one bit of advice *vis-a-vis* the use of foreign words:

Ix-nay the ap-cray.

November 24, 1989

There's more
than one of me

I PROBABLY talk about myself too often in this column.

So today, let's talk instead about Steve Blow. And Steve Blow and Steve Blow and Steve Blow .

Sounds like fun, doesn't it?

I suppose if your name is John Smith or Mary Jones, you get used to the idea that other people share your name. But when your name is Blow, you go through life feeling sort of, uh, unique.

So imagine my surprise when I discovered that there are other Steve Blows out there.

The poor things.

I stumbled upon this shocking information while researching a possible column on Summit Search of Banks, Ore.

Mike Phalen is a mechanical engineer in Banks. He happened to read one day about databases that work like a national phone directory. These directories are used mostly by "skip tracers"—people who specialize in tracing those who have skipped out on their debts.

But Mike had an idea for putting the data to a more pleasant use. "I thought, 'I'd like to look up some old college friends.' "'

Then he began thinking of how class reunion committees are always searching for people. And he thought of how families search for lost relatives. And then he realized he had a business idea on his hands.

So Mike acquired one of the databases and formed Summit Search, charging customers $29 to search the nation for everyone with a certain name. Mike has lots of stories to tell about happy reunions between old friends, lost loves and parted families.

Just for fun, one of the first names Mike searched for was his own—Michael Phalen. "I was kind of amazed to find 20 of them," he said. Then he asked, "Would you like me to search for your name?"

Well, of course, there's only one Steve Blow. And I'm sure all 13 of us thought so.

What a weird sensation to look at a list of yourselves.

One evening last week, I spent an hour or so calling Steve Blows: "Is this Steve Blow?" "Yes." "This is Steve Blow." "What?"

First I spoke with Steve Blow of Edwards, N.Y. That's just a stone's throw from the Canadian border. He was a real nice fellow, but then I think we all are.

Steve is a 38-year-old grocery manager. He said the Blows up in that area are French, having changed the name from Bleau or Bleaux.

I asked if he wished they had never changed it. "I sure do—for a lot of reasons," he laughed. "I have a 14-year-old daughter, and she hates her last name."

What a coincidence! I have a 14-year-old daughter, and she hates her last name!

Then I talked to 34-year-old Steve Blow of Lexington, Tenn. And speaking of coincidences—he's a writer. Well, actually he's a land buyer for the state highway department. But he writes some on the side.

I asked what kind of writing he does. "Outdoor adventures, mostly," he said. "Stuff based on my huntin' and fishin' ."

He hastened to add, "I write by a different pen name. I don't use Blow.'

Why didn't I think of that? A non Blow de plume!

He said he writes under the pen name "Remington Schuller.' Now there's a name! Manly—yet sensitive, too. Like a cross between Remington Steele and the Rev. Robert Schuller.

Finally I talked to Steve Blow of Old Orchard Beach, Maine. He's 25 and tells me there are lots of Blows up that way.

At first I thought Steve was saying something about "our family's lodge." I was hoping I had found the rich side of the family.

Actually he was saying, with a Maine accent, "our family is large."

The Maine Blows are, in fact, successful business people. Steve represents the third generation to work in the family business—Blow Brothers.

It's a portable toilet and septic tank pumping service. "We're the largest in southern Maine," Steve said.

"Our motto is, 'We're No. 1 in the No. 2 business.' "

Proud? I nearly busted my buttons.

November 8, 1992

Hometown hero's
tale still tragic

WHEN I WAS growing up, I loved to hear family stories. Some were funny. And some were really sad. (In fact, my family seemed to specialize in the sad ones.)

But for me, one story rose above all the rest. No other story could match the tragic saga of John Henry Jackson.

John Henry was a cousin of mine—a first cousin once removed, if you want to get technical about it. My grandfather and his mother were brother and sister.

I never knew John, for reasons that will be obvious. But his story made him a major figure in my childhood imagination.

John was Aunt Ollie's boy—the first son among four sisters. And as you can imagine, that made him something of a pet.

The family lived in Alvarado, a small town south of Fort Worth. Actually, they lived on the edge of town, share-cropping in those Depression years on a place called "the Ross farm."

My mother remembers John as a freckle-faced, all-American kind of boy. "He was a big tease," she said.

World War II was brewing when John finished high school, and he went straight into the military. In fact, he was an Army Air Corps mechanic at Pearl Harbor when the Japanese attacked and was cited for bravery under fire.

Family pride in John shot even higher when he was accepted into flight school and became a pilot. John's sister, Hazel Jones, who still lives in Alvarado, recalled how proud all the sisters were when John was first commissioned as an officer.

"We talked him into walking down the street one day while we followed along behind him. We just wanted to see another soldier salute him," she said, chuckling at the memory. "I don't think we ever did see him get saluted."

In February 1943, John was home in Alvarado on leave. He was about to go overseas to "fly the hump"—the dangerous job of ferrying war supplies over the Himalaya Mountains into China.

Though he was a hero in the family's eyes, John was still a 21-year-old kid at heart. Still that big tease. His nickname said it all. Around Alvarado, John was known as "Breezy."

On the Sunday of Feb. 7, 1943—a Sunday exactly 50 years ago today—John drove up to the new air base in Fort Worth and checked out a single-engine advanced-trainer plane.

John had a little mischief in mind. His passenger was another Alvarado boy, Army Air Corps mechanic Dell Shelton.

"The Shelton boy told his mother that he was going to come down and dust off her rooftop," Hazel recalled.

Soon, the plane was buzzing low over Alvarado, putting on a stunt show for the whole town.

An older fellow later told Hazel that he thought about calling the air base to report the low-flying plane. "But," he said, "I knew it was Breezy, and I didn't want to get him in trouble."

John apparently had a particular target in mind for one last low pass—the Mahanay Brothers' service station.

"My brother used to love to hang around that station when he was growing up," Hazel said. "He was crazy over those Mahanay brothers."

John Henry zoomed down low over the station, and then tried to pull up sharply. But he couldn't climb fast enough, and the plane clipped an electrical line.

Witnesses said it appeared that John fought hard to keep the plane under control as it skimmed above the ground. He pulled up just high enough to clear the train station at the edge of town. But one wing struck a boxcar parked on a siding and the plane catapulted into the ground, not far from the Ross farm.

I looked back through old copies of *The Dallas Morning News* last week, and sure enough, there it was—a front-page story headlined "Two Fliers Die In Crash At Alvarado.'

When I was a kid, the saga of John Henry broke my heart every time I heard it—the hometown hero brought down by his own folly.

It still breaks Hazel's heart. "He kind of died with a black mark because of what he did. He was showing off for the hometown folks— that's what he was doing,' she said.

"It was all so sad. I remember at his funeral, the preacher said, 'He was Alvarado's boy.' "

"He was a handsome young man, and we were proud of him," Hazel said. "And I still am."

February 7, 1993

It's very easy to forget
how hard life was

WHILE RUMMAGING around in the garage the other day, I came across an oil spout. I looked at it a moment and thought, "What a wonderful world."

Maybe you never had to use an oil spout. Maybe you never had an old, oil-burning car. But I did, and no matter how carefully I pushed the spout into an oil can, it always dripped and got oil all over my hands and the car and everything else.

I had forgotten all about oil spouts.

They started putting oil in easy-to-pour plastic bottles several years ago, and I promptly forgot that oil spouts ever existed.

That's kind of the way it is, isn't it? We love to marvel at new technology. But once it arrives, we immediately take it for granted.

That oil spout got me thinking about the many little ways life is easier. And since I was thinking of cars, the first thought that popped into my mind was auto air conditioners.

I had managed to forget the misery of those long, unair-conditioned car trips when I was a kid. With the windows up, the car was an oven. With the windows down, it was like sitting in a cyclone. A hot cyclone.

And what about house air conditioners? Remember when it finally got so hot in August that fans didn't help. You would sleep with your head at the opposite end of the bed, trying to catch the slightest breeze from the open window.

Wait, I just thought of another car convenience—cruise control. Now there's a wonderful invention. It allows drivers to nap on long trips.

Icemakers! How could I not give thanks each and every day for that wonderful invention? There is no job I hate more than emptying and refilling ice trays.

Here's another one—coffee pots with automatic timers. It's so luxurious to wake up to the aroma of brewing coffee. (Of course, they only work if someone in the household is sweet enough to fix the pot the night before. And I promise to do better, dear.)

How about pop-top cans and twist-off tops? Remember arriving at the picnic and discovering that no one had a "church key?"

I'm really making myself sound like an old geezer here, aren't I?

Remember when your family got the first "extension" phone? Imagine, two phones in one house! And in colors, no less.

Now we have cordless phones, cellular phones, speaker phones, self-answering phones, faxing phones, two-line phones and even the long-awaited video phones.

I encountered an old-fashioned rotary dial phone the other day. It seemed to take forever to crank that dial around. (One ringy-dingy, two ringy-dingies . . . .)

Nowadays we take it for granted that a clothes dryer sits beside a clothes washer. Once that wasn't so, and every back yard had a clothes line. (And parents were forever yelling at the kids, "Don't swing on the clothesline!") Remember the panic that would set in during a long rainy spell, when the dirty laundry began to pile up?

And ladies, let's take a moment of silence to give thanks for curling irons, electric rollers and blow dryers. Think back to sleeping on rollers and sitting under hair-dryer bonnets by the hour.

I'm thankful for those high-tech cash registers at McDonald's. Workers don't have to read or count. They just push picture buttons and the machine tells them how much change I'm owed.

When I worked at McDonald's in prehistoric times (1969), we took orders and added prices with a pencil. Can you imagine the chaos today if fast-food clerks had to do actual mathematics?

There is so much we take for granted—and I'm not even talking about the big stuff like computers and jet airliners and satellite communications.

I'm talking about latex paint and pocket calculators and string weed trimmers and disposable diapers and VCRs and garage door openers and automated teller machines.

It's also worth remembering that while we take these things for granted, most people in the world don't have them at all.

May 28,1993

God moves in mysterious, but neat ways

IT SEEMS THAT God not only answers prayers, but also manages to do good deeds along the way.

Kyle L. Thompson of Dallas recently went on an Indian Guides campout with his 6-year-old son, Jordan. They went to Camp Grady Spruce, west of Fort Worth.

When they got home that Sunday night, Kyle discovered that his wallet was missing. It contained cash and credit cards and blank checks—"just about everything," he said.

"But I really didn't worry too much," Kyle said. "I just assumed that I had lost it at the camp. I was sure it would be returned."

He called the camp on Monday morning, but by Tuesday there was still no sign of his wallet. That's when the worrying set in.

Kyle's son and 5-year-old daughter, Audrey, certainly sensed that the loss of Daddy's wallet was a big deal. When they said their bedtime prayers, each of them asked for God's help in finding it.

And God went to work.

On the other side of Fort Worth, a husband and wife were having their own stretch of bad luck.

Phillip and Laurie Sterner had arrived in town just a week before. Phillip is a roofer from Denver. But things hadn't been going well there, and so they traveled to Texas in hopes of finding work.

Phillip did manage to quickly find a job. But it would be a week before he would draw his first paycheck. So they used the last of their money to rent a motel room in Weatherford for the week.

And they resigned themselves to skipping most meals until the check arrived.

On Wednesday morning, as Phillip was driving to work, his old '76 Oldsmobile blew a radiator hose.

"I sat there wondering, 'What am I going to do? What am I going to do?' " he said.

An auto parts store was nearby, but Phillip didn't have the money for a new radiator hose. "I didn't even have a quarter to call the shop to tell them I wasn't coming to work," he said.

He sat there with visions of losing his job, ending up even more broke than before.

Phillip noticed a pawnshop near the auto parts store. And in desperation, he removed the radio from his car and carried it to the pawnshop, hoping to get just enough money for a new hose.

"It's amazing how priceless a radiator hose becomes," he said.

But the pawnshop refused the radio. Utterly dejected, he began walking back toward his car. And just before he reached it, there on the side of the road, he spotted the wallet.

Phillip said he wasn't praying for a miracle. "I was really kind of angry," he said. "But when I saw the wallet, I looked up in the sky and said, 'God must have dropped this. I didn't see him drop it. But God must have dropped this.' "

When he saw the cash inside, Phillip said, he heard a voice plain as day say: You've got to give it back . "It was like God was shouting at me," he said.

At that point Phillip struck a little bargain with God. He would give the wallet back, all right, but he would also borrow just enough to fix the radiator hose and get to work. Then he would repay the loan from his first paycheck.

And that's just what he did, borrowing $20 from Kyle Thompson's lost wallet.

Kyle couldn't believe it when Phillip called that afternoon to report finding the wallet—and taking the loan. Only then did Kyle remember stopping along the highway to get snacks from the trunk. That's when the wallet fell out.

Kyle insisted that Phillip take $50 from the wallet as a reward. Phillip said he wouldn't do that, but that he would, if it was OK, borrow a bit more for food.

"Kyle fed us for a couple of days there," Phillip said.

Two nights later, Kyle drove over to Fort Worth to meet Phillip and retrieve the wallet. By this time, Phillip had received his first check and repaid the loan.

But Kyle insisted that Phillip accept a small reward. And so he did.

Now the two consider themselves fast friends. "Kyle is the hero here," Phillip said. "What a nice guy."

"Don't give me any credit," Kyle said. "I am so impressed with Phillip. This has really restored my faith."

A nice trick for a wallet.

October 29, 1995

Family learns about
letting loved one pass

THIS WEEK'S issue of *Newsweek* magazine has Cardinal Joseph Bernardin on the cover. And a jarring headline—"Teaching Us How To Die."

As a society, we don't like dealing with death.

We don't have much patience for sick people, much less dead ones.

When people do die, we rush the embalmers in to make them look healthy again.

Given all that, the Bonner family's quiet, rich experience with death is even more remarkable.

The outline of Bob Bonner's life is a familiar one. He grew up in East Texas during the Depression, the oldest of nine kids.

World War II came along and pushed aside his dream of playing pro baseball. And after the war, like so many other poor boys from East Texas, he settled in Dallas and settled into work.

He took a job selling building materials and eventually started his own successful business in that field, the Bob Bonner Co.

He and his wife, Ellie, raised four children in a house near White Rock Lake.

Bob Bonner's dying—or at least his knowledge of it—began in September. He went into Baylor University Medical Center for fairly routine back surgery.

But tests revealed that he had cancer—and that it was in his lungs, his liver and his brain.

After a brief, futile attempt at treatment, it became clear that death was at hand.

"I have never watched anyone die," his daughter, Cathy Bonner, said. "No one else in my family knew what to do, either."

She credits the nurses at Baylor with helping the family learn to face death with courage. "Nurse-angels," she calls them.

"The nurses really pulled us through. They taught us that our job was to love him, to keep him comfortable and, as hard as it sounds, to let him go."

One by one, Mr. Bonner's bodily systems began to shut down. Even when he appeared to have slipped into a coma, nurses told the family that he could still draw comfort from their touch and their words.

And they said the family might have to tell him that it is OK to die.

Cathy sat beside her father's bed throughout his final night, listening to each deep, labored breath. About dawn, as light spread across the city, Cathy decided it was time for that talk.

Thirty-two days had passed since he was first diagnosed with cancer.

In the *Newsweek* article, it mentions that Cardinal Bernardin turned to another priest, Father Henri Nouwen, for guidance in facing death. The cardinal died last week from pancreatic cancer.

It so happens that Cathy had just read a book by Father Nouwen, *Our Greatest Gift.*

"Daddy," she whispered close to his ear, "I want to tell you about something I read in a book . . . ."

And she began talking to him about Father Nouwen and his thoughts on death. "He says dying is like flying on the trapeze at the circus," she told him.

"You know the flier gets all the glory, all the fame. But it is the catcher who really does all the work.

"The catcher has to be there with split-second precision to grab the flier out of the air. The secret is the flier does nothing. He just stretches out his arms and trusts the catcher will be there and pull him to safety.

"The worst thing a flier can do is try to catch the catcher. It could prove disastrous for both artists on the trapeze."

And she whispered, "Daddy, don't be afraid to fly into your catcher's arms. You have done everything in life you were supposed to do. You are leaving us perfectly equipped to have good lives, too.

"Don't try to grab the catcher, Daddy. He will grab you. Just stretch out your arms . . . ."

Bob Bonner lived a few more hours, long enough for family members to all gather and say their goodbyes.

"At the moment of death," Cathy said, "my father opened his eyes, looked at my mother and did not take another breath.

"It was time for the flier to fly," she said, "and the catcher to catch."

November 22, 1996

Is it tough to learn
new language? Sí

BUENOS DIAS. Hola. Como estan, amigos?

Can you tell I've been taking Spanish lessons? Can you tell I've just said everything I know?

And if you heard my Spanish with an East Texas accent, you'd really . . . uh . . . I just realized I don't know the word for "laugh."

See, that's the trouble with another language. It has different words for everything.

OK, I just looked it up. If you could hear my East Tex-Mex, you'd be *reir* -ing your rear end off.

I'll tell you this about studying another language: It takes all the fun out of grousing, "I wish those people would learn to speak English."

Suddenly you're a lot more impressed by those who have learned English—and a lot more sympathetic to those who are trying.

Did you know verbs conjugate?

Normally you don't have to think about such stuff. You just open your mouth and talk. But with another language, suddenly you're obsessed with first-person singular and third-person plural.

Over and over you go: *Hablo, hablas, habla, hablamos, hablan* . . . .

And just about the time you think you've got it down, the teacher says, "OK, that's present tense. Now let's learn the past tenses—preterit and imperfect."

Hable, hablaste, hablo, hablamos, hablaron . . . Hablaba, hablabas, hablaba, hablabamos, hablaban . . . .

And when you begin to get those, you discover that there's also future tense. And conditional. And imperfect subjunctive and irregular past participles . . . .

And you're finally tempted to scream, in the immortal words of noted linguist Roberto Duran, *"No mas!"*

I guess this is my granddaddy's fault.

When he was just a boy, he hopped a freight and went out to California to pick crops and see some new territory. Well, he came to love the Mexican people and their language.

So when he came home to East Texas, he worked and worked to teach himself Spanish. And he did it so well that he landed a job with the U.S. Customs Service in Laredo.

That's where Mom grew up, mostly. So she speaks a smidgen of Spanish. It was always kind of embarrassing as a kid. She was the only mother on the block who called that slab of concrete behind the house the "potty-o."

Granddaddy was so eager for his children to learn Spanish that he would volunteer to do their chores at night—the dishwashing or whatever—if they would spend the time studying Spanish. And it worked. My uncle Jan became a Spanish and French teacher. And others in the family seem to have a flair for languages.

But then there's me. *Yo . . . soy . . . muy . . . estupido . . . .* My grade-point average in college would have been much higher except for those Spanish classes.

Well, here I am now, trying to get back up on that *caballo* .

In some ways, Spanish is not so hard. A lot of words are nearly the same. Want to try a few? *Delicioso*? Right, "delicious." *Inteligente*? Very good, "intelligent." *Embarazada*? You guessed it, "pregnant."

Oops, sometimes it's hard. *Asistir* means "attend" and *atender* means "assist." Go figure.

And it's interesting how some Spanish words are so similar—*cansado* and *casado* , for example. One means "tired," the other means "married." What a coincidence.

I'm just finishing a year of Spanish lessons here at work. (Gracias, Sra. Davenport.) My wife and I plan to take a little continuing education course this summer. And my real dream is to take some time off one of these days and attend language school in Mexico.

Maybe I feel like I'm honoring Granddaddy's memory a little. But mostly it's just fun.

Did you know that Palo Duro means "hard wood" and Nevada means "snowfall"? Or that Boca Raton means "mouse mouth"? (Do you think they know?)

Oh, and here's a little fun with Spanish. Go into the roughest bar in Amarillo and yell, "This town is 'Yellow'!"

Buena suerte.

May 18, 1997

Incidents raise the specter that we're not alone

YOU KNOW me. I'm a fairly grounded guy. I don't go in for all that woo-woo stuff.

But I may believe in ghosts.

I have heard too many strange, strange stories to say otherwise. And maybe the strangest of all came from a young man named Jett Jones.

I talked with Jett 14 years ago, back when I was a reporter covering East Texas for the newspaper. Jett was 15 then, living with his family in an old plantation house outside Karnack. It's the house where Lady Bird Johnson was born and reared.

Jett was just a typical high school boy in every way—except for his friendship with a woman who had been dead more than 120 years.

But Jett didn't think of Eunice Andrews as a ghost. "I just think of her as a lady who lives in the house that nobody else can see," he told me.

Jett's father, Jerry, was well aware of the ghost legend attached to his home. It seems that in the 1860s, 19-year-old Eunice Andrews was sitting near the fireplace in the back bedroom of the house.

A terrible storm was raging outside, and it's believed that a bolt of lightning must have come down the chimney and struck Miss Andrews. She was found lying by the fireplace, badly burned.

And it's said that Miss Andrews' ghost remained right there in that bedroom.

I called Lady Bird Johnson at the time to ask about the ghost. One of her assistants called me back. "She never saw or heard the ghost," the aide said. "But she said she was told so many stories as a young child that she used to feel a sense of apprehension and unease in the house. In fact, she said she still does."

Mr. Jones told me he decided not to tell his children about the legend as they were growing up there in the 1970s. "And then one day, when Jett was 4 years old, he came up to me and said he had just met a friend in the back bedroom. I said, 'Oh, who is that?' He said, 'You know, Miss Andrews.' "

From that first meeting, Jett continued to see and talk with Miss Andrews on a regular basis. He called her "Oonie"—a variation on Eunice.

"She is always sitting or standing in the room when I walk in," Jett told me matter-of-factly. "She disappears only when I leave the room or look away."

And he said: "She just looks like a regular person. You can't see through her, and she doesn't float around like ghosts in the movies."

Her appearance never changed. "She wears a simple white dress. It reaches to the floor and has long sleeves," he said.

Only once did Oonie scare him. It was about a year before my visit. It was the only time they ever touched.

Jett had been in the hospital after a bad car accident. He was battered and bruised. Stitches covered his face. On the day he returned home, he was hobbling around and walked into the back bedroom.

"She was standing right in front of me as soon as I walked in the door," he said. "I had never seen her look touched or show any emotion other than a little smile." But this time was different.

"A tear rolled out of her eye, and she reached out to hold my hand. Her hand was ice-cold, like touching a plastic bag of ice. She held my hand and said, 'As long as your name is Jett Jones and you live in this house, you will never die.'

"It was really weird. About that time, someone called me from another room. I looked around, and just as I did, I felt the cold grasp release my hand. I looked back real quick and she was gone. That sent a real shiver down my spine," he said.

And that sent a shiver down my spine.

This week I contacted Jett for the first time since that interview in 1983. He's 29 now and married. After several years of living in Dallas, he recently moved back to Karnack to help run the family ranch.

I confessed to him that I have wondered ever since if he was pulling my leg. "No sir, I wasn't pulling your leg on any of it," he said earnestly. "Sometimes it almost seems surreal to me. But it really happened."

He said when he was 16 or 17 he realized one day that he hadn't seen Oonie in a while. And he never saw her again.

"I'm 29 now, and I feel kind of awkward even talking about it," he said.

"But it was real."

October 31, 1997

Some assembly will knock you off your rocker

ALL I WANTED was four plastic washers and an apology.

The plastic washers were to finish the stupid patio glider. The apology was for every poor consumer ever suckered by the phrase "Some Assembly Required."

Yeah, right. How about "Ph.D. Required"?

Henry Ford is considered a genius for developing the modern assembly line. I say the real genius was the sharpie who figured out that you could throw a bunch of loose parts in a box and let the dumb buyer sort it out.

And just to make it fun, they give you instructions translated from Chinese. Barely.

The instructions for the patio glider included this line: "Repcat for oppostite side (Diagram A)."

Yeah, "repcat." And "oppostite." And best of all, there was no Diagram A. Nor was there the Diagram B mentioned later.

The instruction sheet had only one of those "exploded views" of the glider—meaning your head will explode when you try to figure out which arm frame attaches to which seat frame with which M6X70 bolt.

I had almost finished the thing when I discovered that I had six plastic spacers left over—items mentioned nowhere in the instructions. I had to start all over again. Grrrr.

For the final step, one labeled "Important," it said I must put a plastic washer on each side of the "glider bracket longers." Well, I'd never heard of a "longer." But I knew for sure that they had shorted me four washers.

Double grrrr.

That's when I decided I wanted washers—and apologies—from the evil glider people.

But who were they? "Made In China" was printed about 15 times on the box. But company names were harder to find. There was something about "Shianco" and "Shian Int'l Co."

I got on the Internet and searched for "Shian." And I promptly found the home page for the Tiong Shian Porridge Centre in Singapore—"A place for delicious porridge."

From the pictures, I'd recommend the fish head porridge next time you're in Singapore.

A second search turned up Min-Shian Industrial Co.—with an office in Dallas! What luck. I dialed the number, which seemed to be answered in another language. "Is this Min-Shian?" I asked. "No, No," the fellow replied.

We stumbled and fumbled for a few minutes before figuring out that we were both saying Min-Shian. But I was saying "Men-She-Yon," kind of East Texas-like. And he was saying " minshin ," kind of Way Farther East-like.

It was the wrong company anyway.

Finally, on my third search, I hit pay dirt. A Shian office in San Francisco led me to Shian International offices in Virginia Beach, Va.— and to consumer information supervisor Kara Berry.

Ms. Berry was polite but said she didn't have the glider instructions in her files. She asked me to fax her a copy.

I did. And when she looked at that exploded view, she said—and I quote—"Oh, wow."

I was feeling better already. "This is definitely a piece of work," she said sympathetically.

I asked her what "bracket longers" are. And she said, "I don't know. Maybe a typo."

After she had studied the instructions awhile and was as confused as I was, she said, "The guy who designed this puppy is in Hong Kong right now. I'll fax the instructions to him."

Later she called me back. "He's furious," she said, referring to Shian executive vice president Bob Gaylord. "He has absolutely no idea how this happened, but those aren't the instructions he created. They're horrible."

And one more thing. "He doesn't know what a 'longer' is either."

Ms. Berry promised to promptly send four plastic washers. And she pledged that all future shipments of that glider will have new, coherent instructions.

She was so nice, I almost hated to ask. But, uh, what about an apology?

"Oh, sure," she said. "I'm sorry. I really am."

I think she even meant it.

May 8, 1998

Junk drawer holds
a mess of memories

DO YOU HAVE a junk drawer at your house?

Please tell me you have a junk drawer at your house.

I refuse to believe that any home is so well-organized that there is no need for a catchall drawer.

You know, the one with several tubes of Super Glue that may or may not be dried up and various sizes of batteries that may or may not be dead. (But probably are.)

I did something unheard of the other day. I cleaned the junk drawer.

And we weren't even moving.

It was sort of a crisis. We were already late in mailing out Corey's high school graduation announcements. (Corey! Graduating! Can you believe it?) And we couldn't find the box of senior photos bought just for the announcements.

We turned the house upside down looking for those pictures. We even looked behind Corey's dresser—which was like studying geological formations. You could trace Corey's childhood in the sedimentary layers of lost stuff : The Legos era. The baseball card era. The golf tees and scorecards era.

But alas, no box of photos. And so, I bravely faced the junk drawer.

Nothing had come out of that drawer in years except dead batteries and dried Super Glue. But I pulled the drawer all the way out of the cabinet and began to sift through the mysteries contained therein.

Junk drawers are like household compost heaps. You fill them with things you can't bring yourself to throw away. And it turns into stuff you don't remember ever owning.

I know I never had a bicycle lock like this. And if I don't remember the lock, I sure don't remember the combination.

Trash.

Where would I have gotten a note pad from Durham Chevrolet-Chrysler-Dodge in Kilgore?

And I swear I never bought this cassette tape—Sir Mix-A-Lot performing the classic "Baby Got Back."

Hmmm, here's a greeting card that never got sent. "Congratulations On Your Baby Boy!" Well, congrats, whoever you are. The kid's probably married.

Allison was helping me for a minute there. She was just home from her first year of college. (Ali! A sophomore! Can you believe it?) But her domestic mood didn't last long. She picked up a tube of something from the drawer and read the label: "Cat Hairball Remedy."

Ewwww!, she said, dropping the tube like it was a hairball itself.

For some strange reason, the drawer was full of pages ripped out of magazines. I didn't understand until I saw the titles: "The So-Long Cellulite Diet," "The Safe Crash Diet". . . .

The Wife-Who-Tears-Out-Diets Diet.

The drawer contained a lifetime supply of those little twisties. And matches. Why do we have all these matches? Snuffers, On The Border, Benavides, Trail Dust Steakhouse, The Mansion. . . .

There's a real test of class: Did you ever dine at The Mansion and not take the matches?

Some people have class. We have matches.

It's sad to say, but the junk drawer passes for a baby book once your kids reach a certain age. Lots of adolescence keepsakes in there. Like the sticker: "Be Nice To Me—My Braces Were Tightened Today."

Here's a pair of concert ticket stubs from Feb. 11, 1990. Who will ever forget "The New Kids On The Block"?

(Everyone.)

Lori stood in line for hours to get those tickets. Or was that for Debbie Gibson?

Here's an old hospital bracelet from the night Ali thought she was having appendicitis—Sept. 25, 1988. One mention of surgery and she was well.

A jump rope. Half a box of sparklers. The directions to Boggle. A Darryl Strawberry baseball card with badly forged autograph.

A "Hello Kitty" ruler from Ali's Sanrio phase. A '43 steel penny from that summer Corey was a coin collector.

I found a little bit of everything. And threw most of it away. Found everything except Corey's senior pictures, that is.

I finally found those tucked away in the junk cabinet.

You do have a junk cabinet at your house, don't you?

May 15, 1998

Rascals & Rounders

JUST AS mishaps make the best vacation stories, the best columns often come from interviews and experiences that didn't go as planned. Here's a collection of lovable rascals and not-so-lovable rounders—all of whom helped to create memorable columns.

I still laugh when I think about the Ku Klux Klan member who couldn't spell his own title. And the experience of holding Jack Ruby's gun—briefly—will always stand out in my mind. As will the murderous thoughts going through my mind.

One of these columns was the first in what became a long series of columns on shady telemarketing practices. I'm proud to have blown the whistle on some groups raising money in the name of law enforcement (and pocketing most of it).

I suppose I should be grateful for rascals and rounders. They sure make journalism fun sometimes.

A few barbs for Cyclops and his Klan

THE KU KLUX Klan poses a real dilemma for serious-minded people.

One school of thought says it's best to confront their bigotry at every turn. Another says it's best to ignore them as the small, sad lot they are.

I know not what course others may take, but as for me, I say send a shot of seltzer up their robes.

After sitting face to face with seven Kluxers at a news conference Wednesday night, it's clear they are too determined to ignore and too dim to take seriously.

The only reasonable reaction is schoolyard ridicule.

And so they will understand, it's got to be grade school insults.

I figure people are fair game if they call a news conference, put on their pretty dresses and pointy Ku-Ku hats, and proceed to belittle most of the human race.

The occasion for this news conference was the visit from Connecticut of David T. White, Imperial Knight Hawk of the Imperial Board of the Invisible Empire, Knights of the Ku Klux Klan. (If this guy wanted a fancy title and funny hat, he should have been a Shriner.)

The first person I met at the news conference was introduced as "E.C. Robert Beam."

"What does the E.C. stand for?" I asked. "Exalted Cyclops," he said.

Unsure that he was really claiming to be an exalted one-eyed monster, I said, "Could you spell that?"

"Uh . . . ," he said with a look of panic.

As a matter of fact, he couldn't spell it. At his wife's suggestion, he got his official Cyclops ID card from his wallet and read the spelling to me.

Apparently the Klan pecking order is based on belly size. Beam is a person of fairly normal human proportions. The next guy up, Great Titan James Knight, carried a prodigious gut overhanging his belt.

The top dog, Grand Dragon Bill Walton, had a belly like the bow of an oil barge. It was too much load for his cowboy shirt to hold Wednesday night and one snap had given way.

Fashion Note: One advantage of Klan membership is that these bellies were invisible once the men donned their robes. Maybe that's the "invisible empire" they refer to.

When the Klan persons were all robed up, they let the wisdom flow. "We are not a hate group," Knight said. "We love the white race."

White said, "The white culture goes back to the Romans which brought us silverware and the Greeks which brought us democracy."

Right, the foundation of America—one man, one vote, one fork.

Their only goal, they said, is to protect the purity of the white race.

Well, the irony was just too much. To put it nicely, these folks are swimmers in the shallow end of the gene pool.

They are the sort who think deeply about whether wrestling matches might be rigged. The same type you would see at better dog fights.

The point of the White visit and the news conference was a little difficult to discern. Some local recruiting drives were planned, but the weather turned cold. Bigotry has its bounds.

At the Dallas City Council meeting earlier Wednesday, White had intended to read a statement praising AIDS as a plague on gays and drug abusers. But he decided that security at the meeting was inadequate. Wise move, buddy. Annette Strauss might have come across that desk and ripped your throat out.

So, in the safety of the Bristol Suites Hotel, White read his rambling statement to three reporters. A Klan security officer stood guard by the door. He looked like Lurch with a perm.

Before the little get-together was over, the Ku-Kus had insulted everyone from African-Americans to Jews to Orientals to gays to reporters to skinheads to other Klan groups.

As comical as these people were, sitting there all puffed up and proud in their silly costumes, there was also something terribly sad in that room.

I guess we've all got a dark corner of fear and ignorance in our hearts. Civilization is the process of overcoming it.

But there are those who take that darkness, dress it up in robes and hats, and make it a way of life. That's the Ku Klux Klan.

February 10, 1989

Truth and romance
—a volatile mix

BRACE YOURSELVES, believers in True Romance.

And I'm speaking here of True Romance as both a theoretical concept and a regular Sunday feature of this newspaper.

The weekly True Romance story appears on the wedding pages. It highlights the courtship and betrothal of a local couple, accompanied by a photo of the happy twosome.

On April 16, the story of Mary-Jo Moody and Noble Steele appeared in that space. It was so amazing that I vowed to follow up on the romance a couple of months later.

As I said, brace yourselves.

Our story, as recounted in True Romance, begins with a routine business call on March 14. Mr. Steele called; Ms. Moody answered.

The business communication led to casual conversation, then to outright flirtation.

The phone call went on for hours at work and continued even longer at home that night. By the end of the day, they had been on the telephone a total of 12 hours and were joking about being engaged.

"Most of the time when I talk, it's business," said Mr. Steele, a phone salesman by profession.

"He sold me—I know that," Ms. Moody said.

Complete honesty, however, was not part of the pitch on either side. Mr. Steele, 40, described himself as 5-foot-10, blond and blue-eyed. In truth, he is considerably shorter, has brown hair and walks with crutches.

Ms. Moody told Mr. Steele she was 35, undershooting her actual age by a couple of decades. And she neglected to mention her nine previous marriages.

Nevertheless, they arranged to meet at his apartment the next day.

"I was lost driving around his apartments, and in my mind I was saying, 'Noble, come outside somewhere where I can see you,' " Ms. Moody recalled.

"And here I see this little guy hopping around on crutches and I thought, 'That must be him, but it can't be—he's not blue-eyed and blond.' "

"The first thing he said when he came up to the car was "Well, do you think I'm ugly?" and I was thinking "Yeah, you kind of are,' " Ms. Moody said.

But they exchanged a kiss, and their fate was sealed.

On March 21—exactly one week after that first phone conversation—they were married.

And that's where the April 16 story of True Romance ended.

Unfortunately, the True Facts were somewhat different. The relationship came to a stormy end a week before the True Romance article was even published.

"He left on April 9, and I haven't seen him since," Ms. Moody said last week.

Ms. Moody is sounding chipper these days, even laughing a little at the turn of events, but she says the ill-fated marriage was an emotional and financial ordeal.

"The whole thing is a puzzle to me," she said. "The day I married him, he changed completely. He made a complete about-face.

"He had convinced me to quit my job because he said he was rich. He said that taking care of him was going to be a full-time job. He had me getting up at dawn to cook and iron for him."

Though she has not seen him since his departure, Ms. Moody has heard from Mr. Steele in a roundabout way. She got a notice that he had filed a misdemeanor assault complaint against her.

"I was defending myself," Ms. Moody said. "He came at me with his steel crutch. He said it was an aluminum crutch, but it looked like steel to me.

"He backed me into a corner of the bedroom, waving his crutch around. He came at me, and all I could find was a little curtain rod, so that's what I hit him with. I hit him three or four times before he left. I was defending my life."

I tried to get Mr. Steele's side of the story, but he wasn't interested in offering it. "I don't want to discuss it," he said. "That woman is a complete, absolute nut."

Both parties said they are seeking an annulment.

Delicately, I asked Ms. Moody if the one-week courtship and the nine previous marriages didn't make her think the marriage might be risky.

"No, I really didn't," she said. "He seemed so sweet.

"I've found that one of the easiest things to do is get married," she said. "But getting out of them isn't so easy."

June 12, 1989

Contemplation of Ruby's gun
. . . and mayhem

I ARRANGED to see Jack Ruby's gun—the gun that killed Lee Harvey Oswald and forever sealed one of the world's deepest mysteries.

The experience was not, however, the quiet communion with history that I had yearned for.

It was more like a head-on collision.

Jules Mayer, 80, is the independent executor of Mr. Ruby's estate and the gun's cantankerous caretaker.

"Why don't you change your name?' he asked me, moments after we had met. "Blow—my wife says that's the oddest damn name she ever heard. People must laugh at you."

I had picked up Mr. Mayer at his North Dallas law office, along with Dallas police Cpl. J.P. Alonzo. One of Mr. Mayer's stipulations on showing me the gun, which he keeps in a bank safe-deposit box, was that I had to hire an armed, off-duty Dallas police officer to accompany us.

At first, I didn't understand Mr. Mayer's insistence on this extraordinary security measure. Later, it was clear. If not for the officer, I might have strangled him.

"Where did you learn to drive?" "Do you see that car?" "Doesn't this car have air conditioning?" "Why isn't it on?" "Turn here." "No, not here, stupid."

I arrived at the bank frazzled, my comtemplative mood almost dashed. Patience, patience, I thought. The purpose here was to ponder history with Mr. Mayer, Mr. Ruby's personal lawyer and close friend.

Mr. Mayer emerged from the bank vault carrying a white cloth bag. It seemed a solemn moment to me.

"Well, let's see if it's still here," he wisecracked.

He reached into the bag and pulled out a black .38-caliber revolver—utterly ordinary in appearance.

By now, *Morning News* photographer Paula Nelson had arrived, and Mr. Mayer had little time for me. He proclaimed her a "a beautiful girl who looks exactly like my nephew, Miles."

As she took photos, I asked Mr. Mayer, "What model is the gun?" He turned momentarily from the camera lens and glowered at me. "Listen, will you please leave me alone?"

I stepped back and contented myself with studying the weapon cradled in his hands. Two tags were attached to the trigger guard. One, a police property room tag, has been there since the day the gun was wrested from Mr. Ruby's hands: "Date—11-24-63. Arrested—Jack Ruby."

A small round tag dates from Mr. Ruby's murder trial. "Stx 6," it says, a court reporter's abbreviation for "State's Exhibit No. 6."

"Has the handle of the gun always been chipped?" I asked.

"The handle is NOT chipped," Mr. Mayer replied. I could see Cpl. Alonzo stifling a grin.

"Right there," I said, pointing to a missing chunk at the bottom of the handle.

"Oh yeah, one time a reporter asked Jack about the gun and he hit the reporter with that corner. That's how it got broken."

Mentally I measured the distance between my hands, Cpl. Alonzo and Mr. Mayer's throat.

Pressing on, I asked him what memories are evoked by holding the gun. He sighed. "There is nothing I can tell you about the gun except that's the gun that killed Oswald."

I asked if I could hold it. He placed the gun in my hands, then immediately snatched it back. "There," he said. "You held it."

And I'd had it. We left for Mr. Mayer's office, where he continued to berate me. "I don't think you understand anything," he yelled. "All you want to talk about is the gun, the gun, the gun."

Mr. Mayer wanted to talk about his court fight with Mr. Ruby's heirs over the proposed sale of the gun. The heirs contend the gun is theirs to sell. Mr. Mayer says he should sell it to pay off the estate's debt—$100,000 in taxes and his $60,000 in administrative fees.

"The only thing that gun means that I can think of is that it will clear Jack Ruby's taxes and administrative costs."

Finally, wearily, I prepared to take my leave. Only then did Mr. Mayer soften a bit. "Hey," he said, walking me to the door, "You know when I called you goofy, I didn't really mean it."

And I wouldn't really have strangled you, Mr. Mayer.

June 16,1989

The Oukah divines
right to be king

A LETTER to the editor arrived the other day from a Dallas man. It was signed:

"His Royal and Imperial Majesty, the OUKAH, Emperor of Tsalagi (the Kingdom of Paradise), King of the Upper Cherokees, King of the Middle Cherokees, King of the Lower Cherokees, Keeper of the Ancient Traditions, and Supreme God of the Sun."

Call it a hunch, but I had a feeling there might be a story there.

So I rang up the Oukah, and I was not wrong.

His Royal and Imperial Majesty was only too happy to consent to an interview. The Oukah lives with his brother, Prince Edward, on the southern edge of Dallas near Lancaster. (Listed in the phone book under Prince.)

The royal residence is under renovation, however, so we agreed to meet at the downtown library. At the appointed hour, a tall, distinguished gentleman with gray hair stepped up.

"I am Prince Edward," he said. Then, turning to the shorter man beside him, he said, "Oukah, may I present Steve Blow."

I wasn't sure whether to shake hands or curtsy. Later I learned that I did right by shaking. The Oukah hates it when people bow.

The Oukah was born 62 years ago in Muskogee, Okla., as Donald Robinson. But the Oukah also hates it when people call him by that name.

"If someone wants to call me by my personal name, they are not my friend," his Oukah-ness said.

The Oukah was dressed in a dark blue, double-breasted suit. The only hint of Native American attire was a big turquoise ring.

The two brothers grew up hearing their father talk of the family's royal Cherokee blood. But their father never publicly claimed his title as Oukah, or king.

"He was a very private man—never made a public appearance in his life, never made a speech," said the Oukah, who took the title upon his father's death in 1967.

"He said: 'Be patient. Someday people will discover the truth about our family.' "

The father downplayed his royalty, but the son decided to play it to the hilt.

"I realized one day that no one would discover us," said the Oukah. "No one was even looking. No one was even smart enough to realize that something beautiful might have survived."

Prince Donald, as the Oukah was known then, moved to Dallas in 1959. "I was an instant, overnight celebrity," he said.

Old newspaper clippings confirm that the crown prince was in fact something of a gadabout back then. In a 1967 interview in *The Dallas Morning News,* he told our Kent Biffle, "Just treat me as you would any other living god."

But then the Oukah dropped out of sight. He said he was mostly consumed with making a living in various "crappy" office jobs.

"I've lived entirely too quietly for the last 20 years," he said. "Now I am collected, rested and ready to start anew. World, watch out!"

The Oukah scoffed at running for office in the Cherokee Nation. "That would be like Queen Elizabeth running for prime minister. It would be a step down," he said.

Yet the Oukah seems unfazed that almost no one recognizes his reign.

"People say, 'You are a fool.' Yes, but a divine fool. I don't need the support of a large group. I have the approval of God, and I feel it every day."

As we talked, I kept waiting for the Oukah to give me a wink, to signal the joke. But it never came.

Then I watched for some sign of derangement, something that would make this a matter for a counselor, not a columnist. But I saw no sign of that, either.

Finally, realizing that the Oukah was quite serious, I asked what royal protocol he expects.

"You'll notice that when we met, my brother said, 'Oukah, may I present . . .' I do not meet people. I am. People are presented to me. When I come into a room, people are expected to stand. When I leave, people are expected to stand.

"Meeting the Oukah should be a special thing," he said. "Without a little ceremony, you might as well be meeting John Doe."

I never did completely figure out this Oukah. But he's no John Doe.

January 8, 1992

Does this call for help
ring a bell?

WHEN I GOT the second call at home the other night, I told the guy, "Someone from your organization just called."

"Are you sure?" he asked. "I don't think we did."

He repeated the name of his group, and, by golly, he was right.

He was soliciting money for the Texas Police Officers Association. The guy who had called an hour earlier was soliciting for the Texas State Troopers Association.

And just a few nights later, someone else was hitting me up for the Texas Conference of Police and Sheriffs.

This is starting to feel like police harassment—telephone style.

Who could have predicted that our police would become the aluminum-siding salesmen of the '90s?

Of course we all support law enforcement officers. And we all want to fight crime. And that's precisely why this fund-raising scheme/scam works so well.

Imagine for a moment, however, that Officer Friendly on the phone said something like: "Hello. I'm a paid, professional phone solicitor. I'm raising money for a police labor union. I'll keep 75 or 80 cents of every dollar you give. The union gets the rest. A dab may go to charity. And by the way, your contribution is probably not tax-deductible."

Somehow I don't think many people would rush to contribute, but that's the truth behind many of these calls.

Out of curiosity, I called the Texas State Troopers Association in Austin. The telephone solicitor had made it sound like a charity. But executive director Claude Hart made it sound like a union—member benefits, lobbying, legal representation, etc.

"We are a labor organization," he said, "but we are not affiliated with a union."

Mr. Hart seemed a little miffed when I asked about his association's fund raising. Nevertheless, he explained that a telemarketing company makes calls all over the state in the association's name.

The troopers get 25 percent of donations. The telemarketers get the remaining 75.

Last year, he said, the association received about $1 million—which means the telemarketing company kept a cool $3 million in contributions.

You Texans are very generous.

The solicitor for the Texas Conference of Police and Sheriffs had told me that his organization conducts education seminars for officers. I asked for a local association address, which he gave as 1414 N. Washington Ave.

That turned out to be the headquarters for the Dallas Police Patrolmen's Union, Local 588. A secretary explained that the Texas Conference of Police and Sheriffs is the statewide organization of local police unions.

Pasadena police Officer Robert Cissell is president of the "conference." I asked him if that name isn't a little misleading. "No," he said. "If people ask who we are, we tell them. We're union. AFL-CIO."

And what about those education seminars the phone solicitor mentioned? "I'm going to one next week on collective bargaining," Officer Cissell said.

His group also gets a 25 percent split from its telemarketing firm. But that's better than the 17 percent from the last company, he said.

The caller for the third group—the Texas Police Officers Association—had told me that it pays $10,000 to the families of officers killed in the line of duty.

But when I called Cpl. Gene Hagen, who coordinates death benefits for the Dallas Police Department, he said, "I don't even know who that group is."

Five phone calls to the Fort Worth-based organization were not returned. Finally, a secretary said Tuesday afternoon that executive director Dwight Johnston had left for the week.

Houston police Officer Mark Clark is director of government relations for CLEAT—Combined Law Enforcement Associations of Texas. He's blunt. "The public is getting ripped off," he said.

And deciding who is legitimate is getting too difficult, he said. So for now, his advice is simple: "If you get a call, don't give."

February 26, 1992

Bad business manners?
You make the call

IT'S HARD TO imagine that the reputation of telephone solicitors could get any worse.

But one company seems to be trying.

Have you received a call yet from Dental Clubs of America?

Or perhaps I should ask: Has anyone from the Dental Clubs of America cursed and screamed at you yet?

It's a local company that was known until recently as Dallas County Dental Club.

When one of the club's telemarketers called Janeen Rose, she was actually interested in finding a dental plan. "He was really fairly cordial, and I was interested in listening to what he had to say," Ms. Rose said.

The telemarketer explained that for $144, the company would provide a list of dentists offering discount services.

"He said he had a messenger that could come out that afternoon to pick up the money. I said, 'Well, I'll have to talk to my husband about it.'"

The solicitor replied: "What time will he be home? I'll give him a call." Mrs. Rose insisted, "No, that's OK, I'll talk to him."

Suddenly, the solicitor turned rude and surly, she said. "He said, 'Well, so in other words, you're just not interested,' and then he slammed down the phone."

Mrs. Rose called the company back and reported the incident to a supervisor. "In a real sarcastic voice, the woman said, 'Well, tell me something, did he hang up on you just like this?'" And then she hung up.

"I couldn't believe it," Mrs. Rose said. "It was incredible."

When I told that story to Dental Clubs president Gary Aporta, I fully expected him to deny it. Or apologize. Instead, he said: "OK? What's wrong with that?"

I think it's safe to say that Dental Clubs of America has a different sort of standard for professional courtesy.

"We are not rude, and we're not abrasive," Mr. Aporta said. "We are, however, direct and to the point. And we don't take any guff off anyone. We sure as hell don't kiss anyone's butt to get them to join the club."

And what a lovely club motto that would be.

Mr. Aporta said his telemarketers are never rude first. "But if someone starts it, we finish it," he said.

We were having a little trouble agreeing on what constitutes rudeness, however, so Mr. Aporta and I did a little role-playing.

He started giving me the standard phone pitch. And I gave him my standard reply: "No thank you. I'm not interested."

"How can you say that?" he asked. "You don't know what I'm going to say."

"Because I have dental insurance and I don't buy products over the phone," I said.

"Well, that's precisely why we created . . . ," he said, resuming his pitch. "No thank you," I said again as he started to talk.

Suddenly, Mr. Aporta began to shout: "Rude! Rude! You're being rude! Why won't you give me the courtesy of listening to me? Didn't your parents teach you to listen when people talk?

"Did you ever order a pizza over the phone?" he demanded. Mystified, I said that I had. "Well then you do buy products over the phone," he shouted. "So you lied on top of everything else. You lied to me. You were rude and you lied."

It was a very pleasant interview.

The Dallas County Dental Society regularly receives complaints about the company. "I couldn't possibly begin to tell you how many calls I've had from the public complaining about their marketing tactics," said assistant executive director Joan Stacy.

"People tell us they are extremely rude," she said. "They would literally cuss somebody out over the phone if they didn't agree to buy into the plan."

For that reason, the Better Business Bureau gives the company an unsatisfactory rating. "We don't really get complaints about the dental service itself. It's more the rudeness and the high pressure to get you to sign up," said BBB vice president Jeanette Kopco.

Mr. Aporta disagrees, naturally. "We're not rude," he said, "and if you tell people we're rude, you're going to hear from someone who is rude."

(They're rude.)

September 23, 1992

Witness seems like
an expert, but at what?

THE NAME carries an impressive air: Castle Forensic Science Institute.

The setting is a bit more modest: a worn tract house in Pleasant Grove.

It is from this "institute" that John Castle operates, testifying as an expert witness on behalf of people accused of driving while intoxicated.

His testimony earlier this month was instrumental in winning a not-guilty verdict in the manslaughter trial of Jimmy Lewis White.

Mr. Castle told jurors that airborne yeast contamination caused the high alcohol content in Mr. White's blood sample—not the 11 pitchers of beer that he had shared with friends last Jan. 15.

Shortly after leaving the bar that day, Mr. White struck a car, killing Fort Worth police officer John Marcellus.

When I spoke with Mr. White last week, he made a good suggestion. He said I ought to be focusing on the reliability of alcohol tests.

"The sad part is: How many other people has this happened to? People ought to be saying, 'Let's look at these blood tests.' But nobody wants to look at the facts," he said.

To that end, I telephoned Mr. Castle and was promptly invited to visit his "institute" in a neighborhood just off Masters Drive near Bruton Road.

The house was stacked to the ceiling with a hodgepodge of furniture, office equipment, books and scientific paraphernalia. A refrigerator in the living room/laboratory contained both groceries and blood samples.

Mr. Castle appeared a bit in disarray himself. He chain-smoked Marlboros and admitted to looking significantly older than his 47 years.

But he spoke in a deep, theatrical voice and with an air of scientific authority that seemed made for the witness stand.

"In all of Texas," he declared, "there is only one place you can go to systematically and reliably get an expert witness for the defense. And that's me and my associates."

Mr. Castle said he had testified in 1,700 cases in six states— "more than any other defense expert in the world."

When I asked how he knew that to be true, he shot back: "Because I study everything in forensics. I read science. Everything in science—and I mean everything in science.

"There are 1,700 volumes of science in this house right now, and I've read them all."

Mr. Castle acknowledged that the house is an unusual place for a forensics laboratory, but he said it contains $3 million worth of equipment. And he said another $3 million worth of research equipment is in the institute's other facility on McKinney Avenue.

Some of Mr. Castle's pronouncements are in question. He is under perjury indictment in Houston after being accused of lying about his academic record.

He calls it a case of revenge by prosecutors. "My trial promises to be about six months long," he said. "There will be 400 character witnesses alone."

Mr. Castle contends that Mr. White's blood sample was contaminated when a laboratory technician opened a sealed vial. "It has to be," he said. "As soon as you pop the top, it sucks the air in and has to be contaminated."

But proof of his theory is hard to come by. I asked Dr. Elizabeth Todd of the Dallas County Institute of Forensic Sciences about the possibility of such contamination.

"We just don't have any evidence that this occurs," she said.

But after talking with Mr. Castle, I began to feel sympathy for jurors. He buries you in a blizzard of words, making it almost impossible to separate fact from fiction.

It finally struck me that his real expertise as a witness is not in creating understanding, but in creating doubt—"reasonable doubt."

Out of curiosity, I stopped by Mr. Castle's other laboratory--that $3 million facility on McKinney Avenue that he had told me about.

It was empty.

The landlord there said Mr. Castle moved out months ago, taking all his possessions with him.

He is indeed a master of creating reasonable doubts.

August 30, 1995

Give her credit: She really seeks cash donations

A READER IN Rockwall sent me a curious letter she received a while back.

"Hello," it begins. "You do not know me, nor do I know you. This is by no means the easiest letter I have ever written. I put a lot of thought into it. For this is one of the hardest things I ever sat [sic] out to do."

The computer-printed letter went on for a page and a half. But here's the heart of it:

"I do not want to cloud this letter with hard luck stories. I just want to be clear, honest, and direct. I am a lady with a child and I need help."

And then the pitch: "Cash or money orders would be best. On money orders, leave payable to blank. Please send donations to: Waiting For A Miracle . . . ."

Well, you've got to give the lady credit—"clear" and "direct," she is. "Honest," I wasn't so sure about.

The letter contained no names, just a Dallas post office box number. I did a little checking and found that the box was registered as a business under the name Waiting For A Miracle. And it was registered to an address in a residential area of southeast Dallas.

One evening last week, I went to the address, not knowing what to expect.

I certainly didn't expect to find a storybook grandparents' house—a lovely brick home with a gurgling fountain, garden swing and new bicycles out front.

Three cars, a pickup and a camper were parked in the driveway. The camper had a "For Sale" sign on it.

An older fellow on the front porch said he didn't know anything about the letter, but he summoned his grown daughter, Linda. She came out on the porch, took one look at the letter and began to sputter.

Linda tried playing dumb at first, then said, "Let's find a place to talk."

She led me through the nicely furnished house, past the big-screen TV and out onto the covered patio, near where the ski boat was parked.

Linda, 42, began to pour out a sob story about the hardships of being separated from her husband, of living in her parents' home, of trying to help them financially, of caring for an 8-year-old daughter and sometimes three grandchildren by a grown daughter.

"I sent that out in a moment of desperation," she said. "But things are looking much better now."

She begged me not to use her full name, and I agreed. She is working now, and I didn't want to jeopardize the job. But I told her that I also felt she owed an explanation to 700 people.

That's how many letters she sent out—using computer-generated mailing labels.

She said a former boss provided the mailing list and the money for printing the letter. I called that boss and he told a different story.

He said Linda pulled the names at random out of the phone book. And he said she charged the printing to his business address without authorization—and that the printing company is still trying to collect its money.

They at least agreed on the inspiration for the mailing: "The idea came when my boss received a letter about how to make $50,000 in a few days," Linda said. "He had read over it and talked to me about it. It was like a chain-letter thing."

Linda said the printing, postage and mailbox rental cost about $500. And how much did this grand scheme collect?

"I got $5 in one envelope, $3 in another, a penny in another," Linda said, breaking into tears. "And a bunch of cruel letters that called me names."

It seemed hard to know what was true in Linda's strange little story. I don't doubt that she was feeling desperate for money. Her family has lots of nice things and the bills to go with them.

And I'm sure that the chain-letter scheme gave her a brainstorm for making some easy money by mail.

I hope one thing is true. I hope she was being honest when she said those 700 people sent her only $8.01.

Linda sees that as the tragic part of this story. "I was really hurt," she said in a pitiful voice. "It seems like proof that people don't care."

But I saw that as the wonderful part of the story.

It tells me that in a world with lots of very real needs, people still have a pretty good nose for smelling a rat.

September 4, 1996

Maybe there's time, place
for injury lawyers.

I HAVE TAKEN my shots at lawyers here a time or two—
especially the ambulance-chasing, TV-advertising variety.

And I don't apologize. But it's funny how a little personal
experience can change your perspective.

My two kids were involved in a bus wreck back last spring.

I can say that now without my chest tightening up. But there's
nothing quite as scary as hearing your daughter's shaky voice on the
phone." Da-a-a-d, we were in a wreck...."

Allison was calling from a hospital emergency room. She and
Corey were on a church ski trip to Colorado. And on the second morning
there, a dump truck rear-ended their bus.

Thank goodness, all the injuries were minor. Ali got a pretty
good whiplash. She said that the worst part was being strapped to a
stretcher for several hours. Corey just bumped his head, but he got an
ambulance ride out of it, too.

Once we knew the kids were OK, the jokes from friends began:
"Now you can retire!" "Hey, that college tuition just got paid!" "Which
TV lawyer did you call?"

I laughed. But, of course, I had no intention of milking the
accident for money. After all, I'm not one of those people.

We were given the name of a Dallas insurance adjuster,
Crawford & Co., and told to send the bills there. When the two $524.50
ambulance bills soon arrived, I said "Wow!" and gratefully sent them on
to the adjuster. Likewise with the $615 hospital bill and the $41
radiology bill.

The only other claim I made was this: The kids had paid $375
each for their three-day ski trip. And the wreck knocked them out of a
day of skiing. So I asked for $125 reimbursement each.

I sat back and waited for everything to be paid, feeling good that
I had been a responsible citizen.

Then the second notice came on the medical bills. And the third.
I called Crawford & Co. and left a message with our assigned adjuster.
He didn't call back. Soon the fourth and fifth dun letters had arrived.

I spoke to a supervisor at Crawford & Co. who assured me that
the adjuster would call. He didn't.

Now the past-due notices were saying, "Protect your credit! Pay immediately!" I called the adjuster again. He didn't call back again.

On Aug. 12, five months after the accident, I spoke to the Crawford & Co. supervisor and expressed extreme displeasure. He promised to check into it and call me back that afternoon or the next morning at the latest.

He never called.

And I finally began to understand exactly why people get sick and tired of the run-around and call one of those obnoxious TV lawyers.

I decided this whole experience might be worth writing about and began calling around. It turned out that the ambulance and radiologist had finally been paid. But not the hospital.

"This is very typical," sighed Kathy Trauger, a financial administrator at Valley View Hospital in Glenwood Springs, Colo. "This is why hospitals and doctors' offices pull their hair out a lot of times."

Not to mention fathers.

Then I learned that my modest $125 claim for the kids had become completely lost in the paper shuffle at Crawford & Co. Images of that TV lawyer in the army tank flashed through my mind.

Al Ellis is a Dallas lawyer who handles personal injury cases— and absolutely hates the TV ads, by the way. He said people come to him all the time out of sheer frustration after trying to handle a claim by themselves. "If the insurance companies did the right thing, so much of this could be avoided," he said.

I hate to say it, but only when I began calling around and introducing myself as a columnist, not just a father, did my case suddenly resolve itself. The hospital bill was paid last week and the $125 reimbursements are reportedly on the way.

A representative for the insurance company apologized profusely and said I had experienced an unfortunate but isolated problem—not at all typical of most cases, he assured me. He said Crawford & Co. had simply been slow to submit the bills for payment.

I called Crawford & Co. and asked for an interview. At least they're consistent. No one bothered to call back.

September 21, 1997

Juror was a real
trial to her peers

I WAS CALLED away into the service of my country last week.

No, no, I wasn't activated for military duty in Bosnia or requested to stand by as backup geezer for the space shuttle.

Those things would have been easy.

I was actually called into the service of my county. Yep, jury duty.

I have tried in recent years to be philosophical about jury duty. Relax, I say. Take a book. Get herded here and there. Fritter away a few hours and then go home.

Of course, I realize now that my philosophical attitude was based on the fact that I had never ever been picked for a jury. Nor did I expect to.

The conventional wisdom was always that journalists would never be put on a jury. Something about not meeting the moral fitness clause, I think.

But wonder of wonders, on Monday morning, I suddenly found myself sitting on a jury.

As criminal trials go, it was pretty routine stuff—a misdemeanor DWI case in county court.

But it proved to be one of the most interesting (nice word for frustrating) experiences I've had in a long time.

I should have followed the lead of the young man down the row during the jury selection process. He announced his idea of a safe drinking limit: "About a 12-pack," he said.

When everyone gasped, he quickly revised his estimate. "Aw, maybe 10." It was still enough to send him home.

But I wasn't that smart. And before you know it, I was filing into the jury box and feeling a little funny being there—like a kid playing "grown-ups."

The defendant was a 56-year-old Dallas man. And the case was pretty simple. The prosecution presented one witness: The cop who said he was drunk. And the defense presented one witness: The drunk who said he wasn't.

Oops, I guess that's prejudicial language. Strike that, your honor, and let me rephrase the sentence.

The defense presented one witness: The man who said he was in drinking establishments for 10 hours that Friday and had only three or four drinks but not a single one in the four hours before he was arrested.

Yeah. Whatever.

He refused to take a breath or blood test after his arrest. So really our only evidence to consider was the videotape of him performing a few sobriety tests at the county jail.

He wasn't falling-down drunk. But neither was he sober. Counting backward, he skipped from 31 to 20. And when he read a paragraph about Texas being the Lone Star State, he waved his arm like Col. Travis addressing troops at the Alamo.

God bless Texas.

The man testified that he had trouble counting backward for a simple reason: "I have dyslexic."

The prosecutor asked for an example of how dyslexia might affect one's speech. "Well, I might say Dumpty Humpty instead of Humpty Dumpty," he testified.

Hey, you can't get courtroom drama like this on television.

It seemed clear to me that the man fit the legal definition of intoxication—that he was "physically or mentally impaired." And after watching the video again in the jury room, we all agreed.

Or almost.

One woman immediately announced that she would never vote guilty and that nothing would change her mind.

And sure enough, we spent an entire day talking with no effect. Well, there was some effect: The more we talked, the more snide and sarcastic she got.

At one point, she snapped, "It must be wonderful for you all to have such superior judgment."

I tried a new tack and asked if she would have put one of her loved ones in the car with the man that night. She just refused to answer. "I don't need you to clarify the issues for me," she said acidly.

So we all just gave up and made uncomfortable small talk until the judge finally declared us a deadlocked jury.

The man is scheduled for another trial in a month or so. And I'm thinking of writing a new drama about the pressures of jury deliberation.

Instead of *Twelve Angry Men* , I'll call it *One Ornery Woman* .

November 1, 1998